The Wordsworth
Book of Intriguing
Words

The Wordsworth
Book of Intriguing Words

—

Paul Hellweg

Wordsworth Reference

First published as *The Insomniac's Dictionary* by
Facts on File Publications, New York, 1986.

This edition published 1993 by Wordsworth Editions Ltd,
Cumberland House, Crib Street, Ware, Hertfordshire.

Wordsworth ® is a registered trade mark of
Wordsworth Editions Ltd.

ISBN 1-85326-312-5

Printed and bound in Great Britain
by Mackays of Chatham plc, Chatham, Kent.

To My Parents
Mr. & Mrs. Robert D. Hellweg
for
their loving support and encouragement

CONTENTS

LIST OF ILLUSTRATIONS

ACKNOWLEDGMENTS

Many people have been of assistance in the preparation of this dictionary, and their efforts are deserving of recognition. To begin with, I'd like to thank the entire reference librarian staff of California State University, Northridge (CSUN) for their research assistance. In addition, I'd like to acknowledge the support provided by the following individuals:

A. Ross Eckler, the editor and publisher of *Word Ways*, has been of invaluable service. He has given permission to use material from *Word Ways*, and he has provided helpful tips to guide my research. And last but obviously not least, he has greatly stimulated my interest in recreational linguistics by publishing my articles.

Robyn Battle, Marvin Vernon, and Cathy Williams have proofread the manuscript and have made helpful comments on its content.

Kathy Loving has typed and proofread portions of the manuscript and has provided suggestions for its improvement.

Don Fisher assisted in an early stage of the research.

Michael Starr, a colleague at CSUN, helped with my teaching load—thereby giving me time to work on the manuscript.

And finally, I'd like to thank my agent—Anita Diamant—and my editor—Gerard Helferich—for their support and encouragement.

Chapters IV, IX, and X are based on articles by the author that have been published in *Word Ways: The Journal of Recreational*

Linguistics. In addition, a portion of Chapter XIII is based on a *Word Ways* article by A. Ross Eckler and Jeff Grant.
Permission to use this material is gratefully acknowledged.

Paul Hellweg
Northridge, California

INTRODUCTION

I have called this book *The Insomniac's Dictionary* partly because it was born in the dark hours of night during my own periods of sleeplessness. More to the point, it's the perfect book for insomniacs, book browsers, and anyone else with a little time to while away. For one, it doesn't require much in the way of mental or emotional commitment (have you ever tried reading Kafka at 3 A.M.?). And secondly, it's not meant to be read through at once. I encourage everyone to skim and skip around a bit.

The Insomniac's Dictionary presents nearly three thousand strange and intriguing words, all of which are grouped together by categories. By way of explaining why I've chosen this format, I'd like to briefly relate my inspiration for writing this book. It's been more than a dozen years since I first discovered the joys of dictionary reading. From the very beginning, I was amazed by the richness of our language. I quickly became enchanted with words the likes of *pentheraphobia* (fear of one's mother-in-law), *kakistocracy* (government by the worst citizens), and *ailuromancy* (divination by watching the way a cat jumps). I wanted more. I wanted to see all the phobias, all the governments, all the fortune-telling words. It didn't take long to realize I was stymied—there were books that included these delightful words, but none that grouped them together to be enjoyed as a whole. Thus my research began.

The results are here for you to enjoy. Some of the lists are as all-inclusive as I could make them. Every chapter has been thoroughly and painstakingly researched. I cannot claim that the resulting lists are absolutely complete, but I can state that they are more complete than any lists that can be found in any other reference book.

On the other hand, some of the chapters make no attempt to be all-inclusive. Such chapters are intended merely as introductions to their respective subjects. By way of example, our language contains over 20,000 eponyms (persons for whom something is named). Most of these are obscure scientific terms or measurements, and it's obviously beyond the scope of this book to list them all. It wouldn't be much fun either.

Most of the word lists are pretty long, and I've thus chosen to divide them into smaller groups. I admit these subcategories are totally arbitrary—they are a means of presenting the words in easier-to-digest servings and should not be construed as definitive classifications. And speaking of digestibility, I would not recommend reading some of the longer chapters in one sitting. Remember: this book is best enjoyed by browsing, not straightforward reading.

Though it may be hard to believe, all entries in *The Insomniac's Dictionary* are real words. You may not be able to find them in your personal dictionary, and some aren't even in standard unabridged dictionaries, but all have been accepted as legitimate English words by at least one significant reference work.

This book, I hope, comes to you without pretensions. I do not ask that you learn new words to use in conversation, nor do I expect to enrich your writing vocabulary (the world already has its share of obtuse literature). Some people may find this dictionary useful as a serious reference tool, but this also is not my intent. My only hope is that you find pleasure in the pages that follow.

I

LOGOPHILIA OR LOGOMISIA?

A Guide to "Word" Words

I am assuming that readers of this dictionary are logofascinated individuals. So in honor of all logolepts (word maniacs), I am presenting a list of "word" words as the first chapter. There are obviously hundreds of words about "words," but this chapter is fairly short. Each entry, however, is special. The prefix of each is derived from the Greek *logos*, which means speech, word, or reason.

Because of the various meanings of *logos*, this Greek term is the root of numerous modern words which do not relate to speech or writing (for example, "logic" is based on the meaning "reason"). The list that follows is limited to "logo" terms that do in fact relate to the subject of this book: words. Many of these are esoteric medical or psychological terms; thus I have divided the list into two categories. The first deals with "logo" words of general interest, and the second covers the more specialized terms.

GENERAL "WORD" WORDS

Logamnesia: Forgetting words
Loganamnosis: Mania for trying to recall forgotten words

Logolatry: *worship of words*

Logaoedic: Words having a metrical rhythm

Logia: Plural of logion

Logion: Maxim of a religious teacher (or other short "pregnant" saying)

Logo: An identifying statement or symbol

Logocracy: System of government in which words are the ruling power (all talk and no action)

Logodaedalus: One who is cunning in words

Logodaedaly: Arbitrary coinage of words

Logodiarrhea: Rapid, voluble speech

Logofascinated: Fascinated by words

Logogogue: One who legislates about words

Logogram: 1. A symbol used to represent an entire word ($ for dollar, etc.); 2. a word puzzle

Logograph: Logogram

Logographer: A prose writer in ancient Greece

Logography: Art of arranging letters for printing

Logogriph: An anagrammatic puzzle
Logolatry: Worship of words
Logolept: A word maniac
Logologist: One who studies words
Logology: The study of words
Logomachy: 1. Dispute about words; 2. a word game
Logomacice: Logomachy
Logomancy: Divination based on words
Logomania: Overtalkativeness
Logomisia: Disgust for certain words
Logomonomania: Great loquacity
Logonomy: The science of language
Logophile: One who loves words (hence logophilia: love of words)
Logophobia: A strong aversion to words
Logorrhea: Excessive or abnormal talkativeness
Logospasm: Spasmodic utterance of words (stuttering)
Logotype: Type containing two or more letters cast as one piece

SPECIALIZED "WORD" WORDS

Logagnosia: Any speech defect due to damage to the central nervous system
Logagraphia: Inability to express ideas in writing
Logaphasia: Speech or writing defect due to damage to the brain
Logasthenia: Disturbance of that faculty of mind that deals with speech
Logoclonia: Spasmodic repetition of the end syllables of words
Logoklony: Logoclonia
Logokophosis: Inability to comprehend spoken language
Logoneurosis: Neurosis associated with a speech defect
Logopathy: Any speech defect associated with damage to the central nervous system
Logophasia: Logaphasia
Logopedics: (Logopaedics, logopedia, logopaedia)—Study of speech disorders
Logoplegia: Any paralysis of the speech organs

As a parting gesture, here are two recently coined "logo" words. Each is delightful, but neither one has been accepted by a standard reference work. Perhaps in time . . .

Logastellus: One whose enthusiasm for words outstrips his knowledge of them (coined by John McClellan, "Word Ways," August 1970)

Logocide: To kill a word (coined by Dmitri Borgmann, *Language on Vacation* [New York: Charles Scribner's Sons, 1965])

II

THE ALECTOR'S LEXICON:

Words About Insomnia

This dictionary is not for run-of-the-mill word lovers; it's for *insomniac* word-lovers. Thus, just as we first took a look at "word" words, let's take an early look at all the unique terms that describe sleep conditions. Our language contains many words about sleeping; however, I've limited the following selection to words that relate either directly or indirectly to insomnia and other sleep disorders.

The title to this chapter ("The Alector's Lexicon"), by the way, is simply a grandiloquent way of saying "The Insomniac's Dictionary." See below (alector) and Chapter XVIII (lexicon).

I do not mean to imply that you have to be a confirmed insomniac to enjoy this chapter. But sleepless nights, whether they be habitual or occasional, seem to be virtually universal. I've only once met a person who claimed *never* to have had a sleepless night. This chapter is not for him. It's for the rest of us.

SYNONYMS FOR INSOMNIA

To begin with, here is a list of synonyms for insomnia. If you are in fact reading this at 3 A.M., it might be comforting to know you're not alone. Considering the number of words describing the condition, I should think there must be many people thus afflicted.

Synonyms for insomnia:

agrypnia
ahypnia
anypnia
aypnia
cacosomnia
insomnolence
pernoctation
zoara

SLEEP INDUCERS

Here we have a list of every insomniac's heartfelt desire. The following adjectives are all synonymous and all mean "pertaining to that which induces sleep." These soporific adjectives refer to sleep inducers in general, whether they be an esoteric drug or a simple cup of warm milk (or your Uncle Herman's slide show of his latest trip to Fargo, North Dakota).

Adjectives pertaining to sleep inducers:

hypnagogic
hypnogenic
somnifacient
somniferous
soporiferous
soporific

SYNONYMS FOR SOMNAMBULISM

Your insomnia may not seem so bad once you've seen what some people do in their sleep. Here's a list of synonyms for somnambulism, which means "abnormal sleep condition in which motor acts (typically walking) are performed." For some intriguing variations, see *lunastimus* and *somnocyclism* in the next section of this chapter.

Synonyms for somnambulism:

authypnobatesis
autnyctobatesis
hypnenergia
hypnobadisis
hypnobasis
hypnobatesis
hypnobatia
hypnonergia
noctambulation
nyctiplanctus
nyctobadia
nyctobatia
selenogamia (Literally: "wedded to the moon")
somnovigil

MISCELLANEOUS

The following words all deal with sleep disturbances or closely related themes. Again, insomnia may not seem so bad when compared to its opposites. Narcolepsy, for example, is a medical condition in which the sufferer is subject to falling deeply asleep anytime, anywhere. To narcoleptics, insomnia might well seem a blessing.

Other sleep-disturbance words:

Agrypnotic: That which drives sleep away
Alector: A person who is unable to sleep
Consternatio: Night terrors in children
Dysania: Difficulty in becoming fully awake after sleep (opposite of *euania*—see Chapter XVIII).
Egersis: Intense wakefulness
Hypersomnia: Sleep of excessive duration
Hypnodia: Somnolence (unnatural sleepiness)
Hypnolepsy: Narcolepsy

Pandiculation: *the act of stretching and yawning*

Hypnopathy: Narcolepsy
Hypnophobia: Fear of sleep
Hypnophrenosis: A general term for any sleep disturbance
Hypnosia: Uncontrollable drowsiness
Hyposomnia: Lack of sleep; sleep for shorter periods than normal
Hypotaxis: Light sleep
Levisomnous: Light sleep
Lunastimus: Somnambulist who walks about only when the moon is shining
Malneirophrenia: A distressed state of mind following a nightmare (opposite of *euneirophrenia*—see Chapter XVIII)
Narcolepsy: Uncontrollable sleep
Narcohypnia: Numbness felt on waking from sleep
Oneirodynia: Sleep disturbed with nightmares
Oneironosus: Morbid dreaming
Parahypnosis: Abnormal sleep
Parasomnia: Disturbed sleep

Paroniria: Morbid dreaming
Somnifugous: That which drives sleep away
Somniloquism: Talking in one's sleep
Somnipathy: Any sleep disorder
Somnocyclism: The act of riding a bicycle while in a state of somnambulism
Somnolence: Unnatural sleepiness
Somnolentia: Sleep drunkenness (caused by insufficient sleep)
Sopor: Abnormally sound or deep sleep; coma-like sleep

Finally, I conclude with a word describing an act which—though not limited to insomniacs—is nonetheless universal among them:

Pandiculation: The act of stretching and yawning

III

A GLOSSARY FOR PANTOPHOBES:

555 Phobias

Humans, bless our souls, are not perfect. But lack of perfection is not necessarily bad. Being friends with a perfect person—someone who has absolutely no faults—would seem about as interesting as befriending a robot. I assume not everyone will agree with this; however, regardless of your personal views on human perfection, it is difficult not to be intrigued by the degree to which human frailty is reflected in our language. To this end, I present here a list of 555 phobias that have been identified and named (a comparable list of manias appears in the next chapter).

Though many of these 555 words merely reflect spelling variations, this is nevertheless the longest list of phobias to be found anywhere. I have gleaned them from a variety of sources, but primarily from medical and psychiatric dictionaries. Most of these words are thus rather obscure, though I should think many of them express fears that will have a certain familiarity (if they should *all* happen to sound familiar, you might regrettably be a pantophobe—someone who fears everything).

For the record, *phobia* is a noun defined as an "exaggerated fear" or a "strong aversion." The adjective combination form ends in "-phobic," and the noun combination denoting a sufferer ends in "-phobe." By way of example, this chapter may not be for you if you're a *hellenophobe* (one who fears cumbersome Greek or Latin terms).

In the following list of phobias, I have departed from my typical format of dividing chapters into subcategories. Instead, the phobia words are presented in alphabetical order *by definition*. Hopefully this will make it easier to find words of particular interest.

FEAR OF ...	PHOBIA
Accidents	Dystychiphobia
Air (and drafts)	Aerophobia, airphobia, pneumatophobia
Airplanes	Aeronausiphobia
Amnesia	Amnesiophobia
Animals	Zoophobia
Animals, wild	Agrizoophobia
Ants	Myrmecophobia
Atomic Energy (or nuclear weapons)	Nucleomitophobia
Automobiles	Motorphobia, ochophobia
Automobiles (riding in)	Amaxophobia
Bad men	Scelerophobia
Bald, becoming	Peladophobia, phalacrophobia
Bathing	Ablutophobia
Beards	Pogonophobia
Bed, going to	Clinophobia
Bees	Apiphobia, melissophobia, apiophobia
Birds	Ornithophobia
Blacks	Negrophobia
Blood	Hematophobia, hemophobia, hemaphobia
Blushing	See "Red"
Books	Bibliophobia
Bound, being	Merinthophobia

Body odor	Bromidrosiphobia
Bridge, crossing a	Gephyrophobia, gephydrophobia
Building, passing a tall	Batophobia
Bulls	Taurophobia
Buried alive, being	Taphephobia, taphophobia
Cancer	Carcinophobia, carcinomatophobia, cancerphobia, cancerophobia
Cats	Ailurophobia, aelurophobia, elurophobia, gatophobia, galeophobia, felinophobia, ailourophobia
Celts (the people)	Celtophobia
Cemeteries	Coimetrophobia
Changes	Tropophobia
Chickens	Alektorophobia
Childbirth	Maieusiophobia, tocophobia
Children	Pediophobia
China (or the Chinese)	Sinophobia
Chins	Geniophobia
Cholera	Cholerophobia
Choking (or smothering)	Pnigophobia, pnigerophobia
Church	Ecclesiophobia
Clergymen	Hierophobia (see Holy things)
Closed spaces	Claustrophobia, cleisiophobia, cleithrophobia, clithrophobia
Clothing	Vestiophobia
Clouds (or disease)	Nephophobia
Cold	Cheimaphobia, cheimatophobia, psychrophobia, frigophobia
Colors	Chromophobia, chromatophobia
Comets	Cometophobia
Constipation	Coprostasophobia
Contamination	Misophobia, mysophobia, molysmophobia, molysomophobia
Corpses	Necrophobia
Crowds	Ochlophobia, demophobia, enochlophobia

12

Amaxophobia: fear of riding in an automobile

Crucifixes	Staurophobia
Cyclones (wind)	Anemophobia
Dampness	Hygrophobia
Dancing	Chorophobia
Darkness	Achluophobia, scotophobia, lygophobia, myctophobia
Dawn	Eosophobia
Death	Thanatophobia
Decaying matter	Septophobia
Decisions, making	Decidophobia
Defecation (painful)	Defecalgesiophobia
Deformity	Dysmorphophobia
Demons (spirits, goblins, etc.)	Demonophobia, daemonophobia, bogyphobia
Depth	Bathophobia
Diabetes	Diabetophobia
Dining (or dinner conversation)	Deipnophobia
Dirty, being	Automysophobia

Disease	Nosophobia, pathophobia, panthophobia, nephophobia (see Clouds) (fear of a specific disease: Monopathophobia)
Disorder	Ataxiophobia, ataxophobia
Dizziness (or whirlpools)	Dinophobia
Doctor, going to the	Iatrophobia
Dogs (or rabies)	Cynophobia, kynophobia
Dolls (or infants)	Pedophobia, paedophobia
Double vision	Diplopiaphobia
Drafts	See Air
Drink (alcoholic)	Potophobia, dipsophobia, alcoholophobia, dipsomanophobia
Drugs (medicinal)	Pharmacophobia (fear of new medicine: neopharmaphobia)
Dryness (and dry places)	Xerophobia
Dust	Amathóphobia, koniophobia
Eating	Phagophobia
Electricity	Electrophobia
England (or the English)	Anglophobia
Erection, losing during coitus	Medomalacophobia
Everything	Pantophobia, panophobia, panphobia, pamphobia
Excrement	Coprophobia, scatophobia
Eyes	Ommatophobia, ommetaphobia
Eyes, opening one's	Optophobia
Fabrics (certain)	Textophobia
Failure	Kakorrhaphiophobia, kakorraphiophobia, atychiphobia
Fatigue	Ponophobia, kopophobia
Fearing	Phobophobia
Feathers	Pteronophobia
Fever	Febriphobia, pyrexeophobia, pyrexiophobia
Filth	Rhypophobia, rypophobia, rupophobia
Fish	Ichthyophobia

14

Fire	Pyrophobia, arsonophobia
Flashes	Selaphobia
Flogging	Mastigophobia
Floods	Antlophobia
Flowers	Anthophobia
Flutes	Aulophobia, autophobia (see Solitude)
Flying	Aviatophobia
Fog	Homichlophobia, nebulaphobia
Food	Sitophobia, sitiophobia, cibophobia
Foreigners	See Strangers
Forests (or wood)	Hylephobia (see Materialism), hylophobia, ylophobia, xylophobia
France (or the French)	Francophobia, Gallophobia
Freedom	Eleutherophobia
Frogs (and toads)	Batrachophobia
Fur	Doraphobia
Gaiety	Cherophobia
Garlic	Alliumphobia
Genitals, female	Kolpophobia, eurotophobia
Genitals, male	Phallophobia
Germany (or Germans)	Germanophobia, Teutophobia, Teutonophobia
Germs	Bacillophobia, bacteriophobia
Ghosts	Phasmophobia
Glass	Crystallophobia, hyalophobia, hyelophobia, nelophobia
God	Theophobia
Gold	Aurophobia
Good news	Euphobia
Gravity	Barophobia
Greek customs	Grecophobia
Greek or Latin terms	Hellenophobia
Gringos	Gringophobia
Growing old	Gerascophobia
Hair	Trichophobia, chaetophobia
Hair disease	Trichopathophobia
Heart attack	Anginophobia

Heart disease	Cardiophobia
Heat	Thermophobia
Heaven	Uranophobia, ouranophobia
Heights	Acrophobia, altophobia, hypsophobia, hypsiphobia
Hell	Hadephobia, stygiophobia
Hereditary disease	Patroiophobia
Heresy	Heresyphobia
High places, looking up at	Anablepophobia
Holy things	Hagiophobia, hierophobia
Home	Ecophobia, oecophobia, oikophobia, domatophobia
Home, returning to	Nostophobia
Homosexuals	Homophobia (see Monotony)
Horses	Hippophobia
Hospitals	Nosocomephobia
Hurricanes	Lilapsophobia
Ice	Cryophobia
Ideas	Ideophobia
Immobility (of a joint)	Ankylophobia
Imperfection	Atelophobia
Infants	See Dolls
Infinity	Apeirophobia
Injury (or war)	Traumatophobia
Insanity	Maniaphobia, lyssophobia
Insects	Entomophobia
Insect stings	Cnidophobia
Itching	See Mites
Japan (or the Japanese)	Japanophobia
Jealousy	Zelophobia
Jews	Judophobia, Judaeophobia, Judeophobia
Jumping (from both high and low places)	Catapedaphobia
Justice	Dikephobia
Kidney disease	Albuminurophobia
Kissing	Philemaphobia, philematophobia

Kleptomaniac, becoming a	Kleptophobia
Knives (and other sharp objects)	Aichmophobia
Lakes	Limnophobia
Large objects	Megalophobia
Laughter	Gelophobia
Learning	Sophophobia
Left (things to the left)	Levophobia, sinistrophobia
Leprosy	Lepraphobia, leprophobia
Lice	Pediculophobia, phthiriophobia
Light	Photophobia
Lightning	Astraphobia, astrapophobia (see Thunder)
Love	Philophobia
Love-play	Sarmassophobia, malaxophobia
Lying	See Myths
Machinery	Mechanophobia
Magic	See Rods ...
Many things	Polyphobia
Marriage	Gamophobia, gametophobia
Materialism (or forests)	Hylephobia
Meat	Carnophobia
Men	Androphobia, arrhenophobia
Meningitis	Meningitophobia
Menstruation	Menophobia
Metals	Metallophobia
Meteors (and meteorites)	Meteorophobia
Mice	Musophobia, muriphobia
Microbes	Microbiophobia
Mind	Psychophobia
Mirrors	Catoptrophobia, eisoptrophobia, spectrophobia
Missiles (or being shot)	Ballistophobia
Mites (or itching)	Acarophobia
Monotony	Homophobia (see Homosexuals)
Monsters (or giving birth to a monster)	Teratophobia

Moon	Selenophobia
Mother-in-law	Pentheraphobia
Motion	Kinesophobia, kinetophobia
Music	Musicophobia, melophobia
Myths (or lying)	Mythophobia
Name (specific)	Onomatophobia, nomatophobia
Narrow places	Stenophobia
Neglecting a duty	Paralipophobia
Night	Noctiphobia, nyctophobia
Noise	Acousticophobia, ligyrophobia
Northern lights	Auroraphobia
Nuclear weapons (or atomic energy)	Nucleomitophobia
Nudity	Gymnophobia, nudophobia, nudiphobia
Numbers	Arithmophobia
Novelty	Kainophobia, cainophobia, kainotophobia, cainotophobia, neophobia, cenotophobia
Odors	Olfactophobia, osmophobia, osphresiophobia, ophresiophobia
One thing (or solitude)	Monophobia
Open spaces	Agoraphobia, cenophobia, kenophobia
Opinions (others')	Allodoxaphobia
Opposite sex	Sexophobia
Outer space	Spacephobia
Pain	Algophobia, odynophobia
Paper	Papyrophobia
Parasites	Parasitophobia
Parents-in-law	Soceraphobia
Pellagra (disease caused by protein deficiency)	Pellagrophobia
Penis (contour of one's own visible through clothes)	Medectophobia
Penis (erect)	Ithyphallophobia, medorthophobia
People	Anthropophobia

Performing (stage fright)	Topophobia (see Places)
Philosophy (or philosophers)	Philosophobia
Photalgia (eye pain caused by light)	Photaugiophobia, photaugiaphobia
Pins and needles	Belonephobia, enetophobia
Place (specific)	Topophobia (see Performing)
Plants	Botanophobia
Pleasure	Hedonophobia
Poetry	Metrophobia
Poisoning	Toxiphobia, toxophobia, toxicophobia, iophobia
Politicians	Politicophobia
Pope (or the Papacy)	Papaphobia
Poverty	Peniaphobia
Precipices	Cremnophobia
Progress	Prosophobia
Propriety	Orthophobia
Prostitutes	Cyprianophobia
Protein foods	Proteinphobia
Punishment	Poinephobia
Purple	Porphyrophobia
Rabies	Hydrophobophobia, cynophobia, kynophobia (see Dogs), lyssophobia (see Insanity)
Railroads	Siderodromophobia
Rain	Ombrophobia, pluviophobia
Rape	Virgivitiphobia
Rectal disease	Proctophobia, rectophobia
Red (or blushing)	Erythrophobia, ereuthophobia
Relatives	Syngenesophobia
Religious ceremonies	Teletophobia
Responsibility	Hypengyophobia, hypegiaphobia
Ridicule	Catagelophobia, katagelophobia
Right (things to the right)	Dextrophobia
Rivers	Potamophobia
Rods, being beaten with (or magic)	Rhabdophobia

Room (full of people)	Koinoniphobia
Ruin	Atephobia
Running	See Streets
Russia (or Russians)	Russophobia
Rust	Iophobia (see Poisoning)
Satan	Satanophobia
Scabies	Scabiophobia
Scotomas (blind areas in visual field)	Scotomaphobia
Scratched, being	Amychophobia
Seas	Thalassophobia
Semen	Spermatophobia, spermophobia
Sermons	Homilophobia
Sexual abuse	Agraphobia, contrectophobia
Sexual intercourse	Coitophobia, genophobia, erotophobia (fear of painful sexual intercourse: anophelophobia)
Sexual perversion	Paraphobia
Shadows	Sciophobia, sciaphobia
Sharp objects	See Knives
Shellfish	Ostraconophobia
Shock	Hormephobia
Shot, being	See Missiles
Sin (or sinning)	Hamartophobia, harmatophobia, enissophobia, enosiophobia, peccatiphobia, peccatophobia
Sitting	Thaasophobia, kathisophobia, cathisophobia
Skin disease	Dermatophobia, dermatosiophobia, dermatopathophobia
Sleep	Hypnophobia
Slime	Blennophobia, myxophobia
Small objects	Microphobia, tapinophobia
Smothering	See Choking
Snakes	Ophidiophobia, ophiophobia, ophiciophobia, herpetophobia, snakephobia

20

Snow	Chionophobia
Society	Sociophobia
Solitude	Autophobia (see Flutes), eremiophobia, eremophobia, ermitophobia, monophobia (see One thing), isolophobia
Sourness	Acerophobia, acerbophobia
Specters (or mirrors)	Spectrophobia
Speed	Tachophobia
Spiders	Arachnephobia, arachnophobia
Stairs	Climacophobia
Standing	Stasiphobia, stasophobia
Standing (and walking)	Stasibasiphobia, stasobasiphobia, basistasiphobia, basostasophobia
Stared at, being	Scopophobia, scoptophobia, ophthalmophobia
Stars	Astrophobia, siderophobia
Staying single	Anuptaphobia
Stepfather	Vitricophobra
Stepmother	Novercaphobia
Strangers (or foreigners)	Xenophobia
Streets	Agyiophobia, agyrophobia (fear of crossing a street: dromophobia)
String	Linonophobia
Stuttering	Psellismophobia
Sunlight	Heliophobia, phengophobia
Surgery	Tomophobia
Swine	Swinophobia
Symbolism	Symbolophobia
Symmetry	Symmetrophobia
Syphilis	Syphiliphobia, syphilophobia, syphilidophobia
Tabes	Dorsalis (degenerative Tabophobia spinal disease)
Talking	Glossophobia, phonophobia, laliophobia, lalophobia
Tapeworms	Taeniophobia, teniophobia

Taste (unfamiliar)	Geumophobia, geumaphobia, geumatophobia
Technology	Technophobia
Teeth	Odontophobia
Teleology	Teleophobia
Telephones	Telephonophobia
Termites	Isopterophobia
Theaters	Theatrophobia
Theology	Theologicophobia
Thieves	Kleptophobia, cleptophobia, harpaxophobia
Thinking	Phronemophobia
Thunder	Brontophobia, brontephobia, tonitrophobia, tonitruphobia
Thunder and lightning	Keraunophobia, ceraunophobia
Time	Chronophobia
Thirteen	Tridecaphobia, tredecaphobia, triskaidekaphobia, tri-akaidekaphobia, triskadekaphobia
Toads	See Frogs
Tombstones	Placophobia
Tornadoes	Lilapsophobia
Touched, being	Haphephobia, aphephobia, haptephobia, haptophobia, hapnophobia, thixophobia
Travel	Hodophobia
Trees	Dendrophobia
Trembling	Tremophobia
Trichinosis	Trichinophobia
Tuberculosis	Tuberculophobia, phthisophobia, phthisiophobia
Tyrants	Tyrannophobia
Undressing (in front of someone)	Dishabillophobia
Urinating	Urophobia
Vaccinations	Vaccinophobia
Vegetables	Lachanophobia

Venereal disease	Cypridophobia, cypriphobia, venereophobia
Vertigo	Illyngophobia
Virginity, losing one's	Primeisodophobia, esodophobia
Virgins	See Young girls
Void	Kenophobia
Vomiting	Emetophobia
Waits, long	Macrophobia
Walking	Basiphobia, basophobia, bathmophobia, ambulophobia
War	See Injury
Wasps	Spheksophobia
Water	Hydrophobia, aquaphobia
Waves	Cymophobia
Weakness	Asthenophobia
Wealth	Chrematophobia, chrometophobia
Weight, gaining	Obesophobia, pocrescophobia
Wet dreams	Oneirogmophobia
Whirlpools	See Dizziness
Wind Anemophobia	(see Cyclones), anemiaphobia, ancraophobia
Wine	Oenophobia, oinophobia
Wood	See Forests
Women	Gynephobia, gynophobia, feminophobia
Women, beautiful	Venustaphobia
Women, lewd	Cyprinophobia
Words	Logophobia, verbophobia
Work	Ergasiophobia, ergophobia
Worms	Vermiphobia, scoleciphobia
Worms, being infested with	Helminthophobia
Wrinkles, getting	Rhytiphobia
Writing	Graphophobia
X-rays	Radiophobia
Young girls (or virgins)	Parthenophobia

MISCELLANEOUS

Just to make this chapter complete, here are eleven words which end in "-phobia" but do not mean "fear of" something.

Acidophobia: Aversion of certain plants to acidic soil
Calciphobia: Inability of some plants to grow in lime-rich soil
Counterphobia: Seeking that which one fears
Gentianophobia: Resistance of some cells to staining with gentian
Halophobia: Inability of some plants to grow in salt-rich soil
Hydrophobia: 1) Fear of water, 2) Medical term for rabies, hence hydrophobophobia (fear of rabies)
Hypophobia: Absence of fear
Pantaphobia: Absence of fear
Paraphobia: A mild fear
Pseudohydrophobia: Animal disease that has symptoms similar to rabies
Osmiophobia: Resistance of certain cells to staining with osmic acid

CONCLUSION

Here are two last words to top off our look at phobias. I have found the first in a couple of popular reference books, but have been unable to verify it by an authoritative text:

Arachibutyrophobia: Fear of peanut butter sticking to the roof of your mouth

Finally, I want to say that I found myself fascinated by the large number of phobia words discovered while researching this chapter, and I certainly hope you've enjoyed them. But now that it is all over, you might be sharing my wish to see no more. Such a desire would seem worthy of expression, and I thus conclude this chapter with a word of my own creation:

Phobologophobia: Fear of, or aversion to, phobia words.

IV

MANIFESTLY MANIFOLD
MANIAS

Here we have a listing of "manifestly manifold" manias, which is to say that the following collection of *mania* words is "obviously diverse"—nearly three hundred manias are identified. They range from the relatively benign (I'd like to know a *doromaniac*—someone who compulsively gives presents) to the downright murderous (I definitely do not want to meet an *androphonomaniac*—someone with homicidal tendencies). Between these extremes, there are undoubtedly manias that will strike responsive chords in all of us.

When used as a suffix, "-mania" means an "irresistible impulse to behave in a certain way" or showing an "abnormal interest" in something. The adjective combination form is "-maniacal," and the noun combination for a person thus afflicted ends in "-maniac."

Altogether, 277 manias (the largest list in print anywhere) are categorized and defined below.

TYPES OF MANIAS

Manias can be moderate or extreme, they can focus on one or several subjects, and they can be accompanied by delirium. To begin our look at mania words, here's a list of the different forms mania can take:

Acromania: Mania marked by great motor activity
Amenomania: Psychosis with agreeable hallucinations

Cheromania: Mania characterized by exaltation
Desanimania: Mindless insanity
Esthesiomania: Insanity with perversion of the senses
Hypermania: Intense mania
Hypolepsiomania: Monomania (fixation on a single subject)
Hypomania: Moderate mania
Hysteromania: Hysterical mania (also nymphomania)
Monomania: Psychosis on a single subject
Oligomania: Psychosis on a few subjects
Pathomania: Mania without delirium
Phrenomania: Delirious mania
Schizomania: A mixture of schizophrenia and manic symptoms
Stupemania: Manic stupor
Submania: Hypomania (mania of a moderate type)

WORDY MANIAS

I assume that anyone reading this is likely to be intrigued by unusual words. For our first look at specific manias, I am therefore grouping together all those which relate to the subject of words (either in written or oral format).

Coprolalomania: The use of foul language
Graphomania: Morbid desire for writing
Hellenomania: Using cumbersome Greek or Latin terms instead of readily understandable English words
Klazomania: Compulsory shouting
Lalomania: Abnormal interest in speech
Logomania (or logomonomania): Overtalkativeness
Metromania: Mania for writing verses
Onomatomania: Mental derangement with regard to words (inability to recall a certain word, attaching special significance to a word, and so forth)
Scribblemania (or scribbleomania): Mania for scribbling
Scribomania: Writing a long succession of unconnected words
Typomania: Mania for writing for publication
Verbomania: Morbid talkativeness

MANIAS ASSOCIATED WITH
PHYSICAL OBJECTS

The following list presents those manias which relate to money, possessions, or other tangible objects:

Agyiomania: Abnormal interest in streets
Amaxomania: Mania for being in vehicles
Arithomania: Compulsive desire to count objects
Ballistomania: Abnormal interest in bullets
Bibliomania: Abnormal interest in books
Bibliokleptomania: Kleptomania for books
Cresomania: Delusion of possessing great wealth
Cyclomania: Mania for bicycling
Decalomania (or decalcomania): Craze for or process of using decals
Doramania: Abnormal interest in fur
Doromania: Compulsive desire to give presents
Gephyromania: Compulsive desire to cross bridges
Kleptomania (also klopemania, cleptomania): Neurotic impulse to steal, especially without economic motive
Oniomania: Mania for buying things
Plutomania: Abnormal interest in possessing great wealth
Potichomania: Craze for or process of imitating porcelain by coating glass vessels
Squandermania: Mania to spend money lavishly
Timbromania: Abnormal interest in postage stamps

MANIAS FOR THE NATURALIST

If you are fascinated by the natural world, then you will likely enjoy the following list of manias. They all relate to plants, animals, natural phenomena, and similar aspects of our world.

Agoramania: Abnormal interest in open spaces
Ailuromania: Abnormal interest in cats
Anthomania: Obsession for flowers

Apimania: Obsession for bees
Chionomania: Obsession for snow
Cremnomania: Abnormal interest in cliffs
Cynomania: Obsession for dogs
Empresiomania: Pyromania (abnormal interest in fire)
Entomomania: Obsession for insects
Florimania: Mania for flowers
Heliomania: Abnormal interest in the sun
Hippomania: Obsession for horses
Hydromania: Morbid craving for water
Hylomania: Abnormal interest in woods
Ichthyomania: Obsession for fish
Musomania: Abnormal interest in mice
Nautomania: Morbid fear of ships or water
Noctimania: Abnormal interest in nights
Ophidiomania: Obsession for reptiles
Ornithomania: Abnormal interest in birds
Photomania: Abnormal interest in light
Pyromania: Compulsion to set fires
Thalassomania: Abnormal interest in the sea
Zoomania: Morbid love of animals

EROTIC MANIAS

Though few of us will likely so admit, erotic manias are the ones we seem to find the most fascinating.

Aedoeomania: Nymphomania
Aidoiomania: Abnormal sexual desire
Andromania: Nymphomania
Aphrodisiomania: Erotomania (preoccupation with sexuality)
Chiromania: Morbid impulse to masturbate
Clitoromania: Nymphomania
Cretomania: Satyromania
Cytheromania: Nymphomania
Edeomania: Abnormal interest in genitals

Erotographomania: Abnormal interest in erotic literature
Erotomania (or Eroticomania): Preoccupation with sexuality
Estromania: Nymphomania
Flagellomania: Erotic pleasure derived from whipping or being whipped
Gymnomania: Abnormal interest in nakedness
Gynecomania: Satyromania
Hedonomania: Compulsive pursuit of pleasure
Hysteromania: Nymphomania (also any hysterical mania)
Lagneuomania: Sadism in males
Machlaenomania: Masochism in women
Mentulomania: Abnormal interest in the penis
Nudomania: Abnormal interest in nudity
Nymphomania: Exaggerated sexual desire in a female
Oestromania: Nymphomania
Orchidomania: Abnormal interest in testicles
Pornographomania: Abnormal interest in pornography
Satyromania: Exaggerated sexual desire in a male
Uteromania: Nymphomania

WORDS OF WANDERLUST

I've long suspected that many of us are repressed planomaniacs (see below)—at least I know this mania appeals not only to myself but also to most of my friends and acquaintances. Thus this is my favorite list, and I hope you will also find these manias interesting.

The following words relate to either wanderlust or its opposite (homesickness):

Agromania: Morbid passion for solitude or for wandering in open fields
Drapetomania: Mania to run away
Dromomania: Compulsive traveling
Ecdemomania (also ecdemonomania, ecdemiomania): Mania to wander
Erotodromomania: Abnormal impulse to travel to escape a painful sexual situation

29

Dromomania: *love of traveling*

Nostomania: Mania to return home
Oikomania: Abnormal desire to be at home
Paratereseomania (or parateresiomania): Mania for seeing new sights
Philopatridomania: Homesickness
Planomania: Impulse to wander from home and throw off the restraints of society
Poriomania: Wanderlust
Siderodromomania: Abnormal interest in traveling by railroad

INTEREST IN SPECIFIC COUNTRIES

Closely related to the traveling manias above are those that refer to an excessive interest in the customs or culture of a particular country. My apologies to anyone obsessed with the customs of a country not listed below, but these are the only specific-country manias that have been identified and named.

For the record, all of these manias are spelled with a capital first letter.

MANIA	COUNTRY OF INTEREST
Americomania	America
Anglomania	England
Chinamania	China
Francomania	France
Gallomania	France
Germanomania	Germany
Grecomania	Greece
Italomania	Italy
Russomania	Russia
Teutonomania (or Teutomania)	Germany
Turkomania	Turkey

MEDICAL MANIAS

The manias in this list are a little more esoteric than some of the others we've seen. Most relate to either the abuse of a particular drug or else to a form of insanity associated with a specific disease. The medical manias are:

Antipyrinomania: Addiction to antipyrine (a coal tar derivative)
Bromomania: Mania caused by use of bromine
Chloralomania: Addiction to chloral (alcohol and chlorine)
Choleromania: Mania sometimes exhibited by victims of cholera
Cocainomania: Insanity with delusions accompanying excessive use of cocaine
Ergasiomania: Undue eagerness to perform surgery (also, overeagerness to be at work)
Etheromania: Addiction to ether
Heroinomania: Addiction to heroin

31

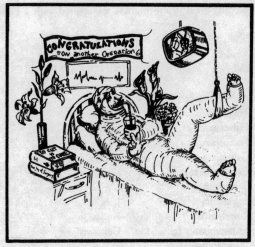

Tomomania: *abnormal interest in undergoing surgery*

Hydrargyromania: Mental disorder due to mercury poisoning

Hydrodipsomania: Epileptic condition characterized by attacks of insatiable thirst

Letheomania: Abnormal interest in narcotics

Medicomania: Mania that appears as a symptom of a disease

Morphinomania (or morphiomania): Morphine addiction

Narcomania: Uncontrollable desire for narcotics

Narcosomania: Insane craving for narcosis (unconsciousness produced by a drug)

Oophoromania: Psychosis associated with ovarian disease

Oothecomania: Oophoromania

Opiomania: Addiction to opium

Ovariomania: Oophoromania

Pharmacomania: Uncontrollable desire to take or administer medicines

Phlebotomomania: Mania for bloodletting as a curative measure

Phthisiomania: Abnormal interest in tuberculosis

Maieusiomania: Puerperal (period of time and/or state of the mother following childbirth) psychosis

Nosomania: Incorrect belief of a patient that he has some special disease

Strychninomania (or strychnomania): Mental aberration due to strychnine poisoning

Syphilomania: Delusion of being infected with syphilis

Thyroidomania: Mental disorder associated with hyperthyroidism

Tocomania: Puerperal psychosis (see Maieusiomania)

Tomomania: Abnormal interest in surgery

Toxicomania: Intense desire for poisons, narcotics, or intoxicants

Tuberculomania: Tuberculosis

Typhomania: Delirium commonly caused by typhoid fever

ALCOHOL ABUSE

The next few sections are rather short, but they list unique manias that are deserving of separate consideration. The first short list relates to alcohol and its abuse:

Alcoholomania: Abnormal interest in alcohol

Dipsomania: Alcoholism

Methomania: Morbid desire for alcoholic beverages

Oinomania (also Oenomania, Enomania): Abnormal interest in wine

Posiomania: Dipsomania

Potomania: Abnormal desire to drink

Pototromomania: Delirium tremens

Tromomania: Delirium tremens

FOOD MANIAS

Some people are gourmets, others are merely gourmands, but most are genuinely interested in their food. The following manias refer to a subject that has a certain obvious appeal. Food manias:

Phagomania: Insatiable craving for food

Opsomania: A craving for a particular food

Oreximania: Enormous increase in food intake due to fear of becoming thin

Sitomania (or sitiomania): Excessive hunger

MUSICAL MANIAS

If you're a would-be Fred Astaire, then one of the following might sound familiar:

Choreomania (or choromania): Excessive desire to dance
Dinomania: Mania for dancing
Melomania: Inordinate passion for music
Musicomania: Abnormal interest in music
Orchestromania: Mania for dancing

RELIGIOUS MANIAS

Some etymologists claim that the word "religion" is based on "relego," Latin for "read over again." Most scholars disagree with this derivation; however, it might be in keeping with the "spirit" of religion to read through this list twice.

Enosimania: Belief that one has committed an unpardonable sin
Entheomania: Religious insanity
Hamartomania: Abnormal interest in sin
Hieromania: Abnormal interest in priests
Iconomania: Infatuation with icons, whether as objects of devotion or as works of art
Idolomania: Abnormal interest in idols
Parousiamania: Preoccupation with the second coming of Christ
Sebastomania: Religious insanity
Theomania: Belief that one is God
Uranomania: Delusion that one is of divine or celestial origin

HOMICIDAL MANIAS

Personally, I'm delighted this is a small category: I certainly hope there aren't many of the following maniacs running around.

Androphonomania: Insanity marked by homicidal tendencies
Dacnomania: Mania to kill
Homicidomania: Mania to kill
Phonomania: Insanity marked by homicidal tendencies

MISCELLANEOUS

The following list is quite long, but these words have defied my attempts at categorization. There are nonetheless some real gems here: among my personal favorites are ecomania, gigmania, and paramania (see below). Should you not like my favorites, do not fear—there is bound to be something here to delight everyone.

Ablutomania: Abnormal interest in washing or bathing
Abulomania (or aboulomania): Psychosis characterized by lack of will power
Automania: Preoccupation with suicide
Autophonomania: Preoccupation with suicide
Bruxomania: Compulsive grinding of one's teeth
Brycomania: Bruxomania
Cacodemonomania (or cacodaemononomania): Delusion of being possessed by evil spirits
Callomania: Delusion of personal beauty
Catabythismomania: Impulse to commit suicide by drowning
Catapedamania: Impulse to jump from high places
Clinomania: Abnormal desire for bed rest
Cratomania: Monomania of power and superiority
Dantomania: Abnormal interest in Dante
Demomania: Abnormal interest in crowds
Demonomania: Delusion of being possessed by devils

Dysmorphomania: Abnormal dread of deformity (particularly in others)

Ecomania (or eciomania): Being domineering toward members of the family but humble toward those in authority

Egomania: Abnormal interest in one's self

Eleutheromania: Abnormal enthusiasm for freedom

Emetomania: Morbid impulse to vomit

Empleomania: Compulsive desire to be employed in public offices

Eremiomania: Abnormal interest in stillness

Ergomania: Compulsion to be constantly at work

Erythromania: Excessive and uncontrollable blushing

Gamomania (or gamonomania): Abnormal interest in marriage

Gigmania: Worshipping smug respectability as the great object of life

Habromania: Morbid gaiety

Hypnomania: Abnormal interest in sleep

Kainomania: Abnormal interest in novelty

Kathisomania: Abnormal interest in sitting

Kinesomania: Abnormal interest in movement

Krauomania: Tic marked by rhythmic movements

Lycomania: Delusion of being a wolf

Lypemania: Profound melancholy

Macromania: Delusion that parts of one's body are larger than they really are

Megalomania: Delusion of self-importance

Mesmeromania: Insane reliance on mesmerism (hypnosis)

Micromania: Delusion that one's body has become small, or that parts of it are missing

Mythomania: Compulsion to lie or exaggerate

Necromania: Morbid attraction to corpses

Ochlomania: Abnormal interest in crowds

Oicomania (or oikiomania): Ecomania (see above)

Onychotillomania: Neurotic picking of the nails

Paramania: Manifesting joy by complaining

Peotillomania: Pseudomasturbation (uncontrollable constant pulling of the penis)

Phaneromania: Compulsion to pick at an abnormal growth on the skin

Phronemomania: Abnormal interest in thinking

Politicomania: Abnormal interest in politics

Processomania: Mania for litigation

Pseudomania (or pseudonomania): Propensity to make false statements

Sophomania: Irrational belief in one's own great wisdom

Symmetromania: Abnormal interest in symmetry

Thanatomania: Abnormal interest in death

Theatromania: Mania for the theatre

Titillomania: Uncontrollable compulsion to scratch

Trichokryptomania: Trichorrhexomania (see below)

Trichomania: Trichotillomania (see below)

Trichorrhexomania: Impulse to pinch off one's own hair with the fingernails

Trichotillomania: Impulse to pull out one's own hair

Tristimania (or tristemania): Melancholy

Xenomania: Excessive interest in foreign customs

BOTANICAL MANIAS

After reading through the above list of manias, you might have been left with the impression that humans are certainly a crazy species. In which case, it might be refreshing to consider that we're not the only ones who suffer from manias—as can be seen in the following list of manias peculiar to the plant kingdom. Now, if you know someone who *does* have one of the following, then I should think that individual is genuinely beyond help.

Plant manias:

Bracteomania: Excessive production of bracts (a type of leaf)

Carpomania: Excessive fruit production

Ceratomania: Abnormal production of hooded flowers

Petalomania: Metamorphosis of stamens into petals

Phyllomania: Excessive production of leaves

NON-MANIAS

In the course of my research, I've found five words which end in "-mania" but which do not refer to a "mania." For the sake of completeness, the five non-mania words are:

Amania: Gold coin of Afghanistan
Dalmania: A genus of trilobites
Germania: Pertaining to Germany
Guzmania: A genus of tropical American herbs
Leishmania: A genus of flagellate protozoans

Finally, if you absolutely did not enjoy a single mania word above, then perhaps this last entry is for you:

Misomania: Hatred of everything

V

OMNICIDAL MANIACS:

A Guide to "Killing" Words

Death and killing are distasteful. Nonetheless, many of the compound words ending in "-cide" (to kill) are fascinating. We are all familiar with some of the more common forms: homicide, suicide, and so forth. But close to 200 other "-cide" words can be found by browsing through a variety of dictionaries. This is just what I have done, and the results are presented here.

Unless otherwise noted, words ending in "-cide" can either denote a killer or the act of killing. By way of example, "uxoricide" can refer either to: 1) a husband who murders his wife or 2) the act of a wife being murdered by her spouse.

Altogether, 197 "-cide" words are defined below. They are divided into six categories—people, the mind, flora and fauna, insects, medical terms—and the ubiquitous "miscellaneous."

PEOPLE

To begin our look at "-cide" words, here is a list of those that have a way of catching our eye, words about the killing of people, whether they be friends, relatives, or strangers. Some are rather whimsical, but most are quite serious and, unfortunately, all too common.

Words related to the killing of people:

"-CIDE" WORD	KILLER/KILLING OF A (AN) ...
Aborticide	Fetus
Amicicide	Friend
Brahminicide (or Brahmanicide)	Brahmin
Czaricide	Czar
Episcopicide	Bishop
Femicide	Woman
Feticide (or foeticide)	Fetus
Filicide	Son or daughter
Fratricide	Brother or sister
Genocide	Racial, political, or cultural group
Gynecide (or gynaecide)	Woman
Hereticide (or heretocide)	Heretic
Hericide	Lord or master
Homicide	Man; person
Hospiticide	Guest or host
Hosticide	Enemy
Infanticide	Infant
Mariticide	Husband
Matricide	Mother
Modernicide	Modernist (person with modern views)
Nepoticide	Favorite
Parenticide	Parent
Parricide	Parent or other close relative
Patricide	Father
Philosophicide	Philosopher (or philosophy)
Populicide	All the people
Prolicide	Child (one's own)
Regicide	King
Selfcide	Oneself

Senicide	Old men (especially as a tribal custom)
Sororicide	Sister
Sparticide (capitalized)	Member of the German Spartacus party
Suicide	Oneself
Tyrannicide	Tyrant
Uxoricide	Wife
Vaticide	Prophet or a poet
Viricide	Man (especially a husband)

THE MIND

There is in fact a word that means "to kill the mind." This section includes it, as well as several closely related "-cide" words—those that describe the destruction of ideas, principles, and so forth.

"-CIDE" WORD	KILLER/KILLING OF A (AN) ...
Ethnocide	Culture
Facticide	Facts (distortion of the truth)
Famicide	Someone's reputation
Fideicide	Faith
Legicide	Laws
Liberticide	Liberty
Logocide	Words (see Chapter I)
Menticide	The mind (i.e., brainwashing)
Philosophicide	Philosophy (or philosophers)
Verbicide	Words (a liar, book-burner, or someone who misuses words)

FLORA AND FAUNA

People and ideas are far from being the only victims of our destruction—plants and animals are also killed. Sometimes this meets with our approval and sometimes not. But language is neutral, and the following terms imply neither approval nor disapproval.

Words about the killing of plants and animals:

"-CIDE" WORD	KILLER/KILLING OF A (AN) ...
Apricide	Boars
Avicide	Birds
Birdicide	Birds
Bovicide	Oxen
Canicide	Dogs
Cervicide	Deer
Ceticide	Whales
Elephanticide	Elephants
Felicide	Cats
Floricide	Flowers
Gallicide	Fowls
Gallinicide	Chickens or turkeys
Herbicide	Plants
Herpecide (or herpicide)	Reptiles
Hiricide	Goats
Hirudicide	Leeches
Lupicide	Wolves
Macropocide	Kangaroos
Molluscacide	Snails and related molluscs
Muricide	Mice
Perdricide	Partridges
Phytocide	Plants
Piscicide	Fish
Poultrycide	Poultry
Raticide	Rats
Rodenticide	Rodents
Sealicide	Seals
Serpenticide	Serpents
Sparrowcide	Sparrows
Talpicide	Moles
Tauricide	Bulls
Ursicide	Bears

42

Vaccicide	Cows
Verminicide	Vermin
Vulpicide	Fox
Weedicide	Weeds

INSECTS

Finally we come to a subject about which few people have any qualms. With the exception of those who believe in the doctrine of ahimsa (see Chapter XVIII), we are usually happy to help most insects into the next world. The following is a list of those agents we employ to that end:

"-CIDE" WORD	*KILLER/KILLING OF...*
Acaricide	Mites
Adulticide	Adult insects (as opposed to larvae)
Anophelicide	Anopheles mosquitoes
Aphidicide (or aphicide)	Aphids
Apicide	Bees
Arachnidcide	Arachnids (spiders, scorpions, etc.)
Cimicide	Bedbugs
Culicicide (or culicide)	Gnats and mosquitoes
Formicide (or formicicide)	Ants
Imagocide (or imagicide)	Adult insects (especially mosquitoes)
Insecticide	Insects
Larvicide	Larvae
Lousicide	Lice
Miticide	Mites
Mosquitocide	Mosquitoes
Muscacide (or muscicide)	Flies
Ovicide	Insect eggs
Pediculicide	Lice
Pesticide	Pests
Pulicide (or pulicicide)	Fleas

Tickicide	Ticks
Vespacide	Wasps

MEDICAL TERMS

Here's another list of "-cide" words that we rarely find objectionable. All the following are medical terms describing agents that kill microbes, germs, parasites, and related unwelcome infectious organisms.

"-CIDE" WORD	*KILLER/KILLING OF...*
Anthracocide	Anthrax bacteria
Ascaricide	Roundworms
Bacillicide	Bacilli
Bactericide (also bacteriacide, bacteriocide)	Bacteria
Cytocide	Cells
Epizoicide	Animal parasites
Febricide	Fever (i.e., reduces a fever)
Filaricide	Filariae (roundworms)
Fungicide	Spores
Gametocide	Malarial parasites
Germicide	Germs
Globulicide	Blood corpuscles
Gonococcide (or gonoccocide)	Gonococci (the causative agent of gonorrhea)
Helminthicide	Intestinal worms
Leukocide (or leucocide)	Leukocytes (white blood corpuscles, etc.)
Lumbricide	Roundworms
Microbicide	Microbes
Nematocide (or nematicide, nemacide)	Nematode worms (roundworm, ect.)
Oxyuricide	Worms of the genus Oxyuris
Parasiticide	Parasites
Plasmodicide	Malarial parasites
Protozoacide	Protozoans

Scabicide (or scabieticide)	Organisms which cause scabies
Schistosomacide (or schistosomicide)	Schistosomes (blood flukes)
Schizonticide	Malarial parasites
Spermicide (also spermatocide, spermatozoicide)	Sperm
Spirillicide	Spirilla (a type of bacteria)
Spirocheticide (or spirochaeticide)	Spirochetes (a type of parasitical bacteria)
Sporicide	Spores
Staphylocide (also staphylococcide, staphylococcicide)	Organism which causes staph infections
Streptococcicide	Streptococci (a type of bacteria)
Taenicide (also taeniacide, teniacide, tenicide)	Tapeworms
Toxicide (or toxinicide)	Toxins (i.e., a drug capable of overcoming toxic agents)
Treponemicide	Parasitical bacteria
Trichomonacide	Parasite that causes trichomoniasis (diarrhea)
Trypanocide (or trypanosomacide)	Organism that causes sleeping sickness
Tuberculocide	Tuberculosis bacilli
Tumorcide	Cancer cells
Vermicide	Intestinal worms
Viruscide (or virucide)	Viruses

MISCELLANEOUS

Here's all the remaining "-cide" words that do not fit into any of the above categories. But last, of course, is not least. If you'll pardon the pun, some of these words are real "killers."

Miscellaneous "-cide" words:

Algaecide (or algicide): That which kills algae
Amebacide (also amebicide, amoebicide): That which kills amebae

Tomecide: *literally, to kill a book*

Autocide: To kill someone with a motor vehicle
Biocide: 1) Gradual destruction of bodily tissues as the result of unhealthy self-indulgence; 2) the destruction of life in general
Christicide (capitalized): The killing of Christ
Deicide: To kill a god
Ecocide: Destruction of the natural world
Giganticide: To kill giants
Monstricide: To kill a monster
Mundicide: To destroy the entire world
Petracide: The destruction of ancient stone buildings or monuments
Prenticecide: An apprentice killer
Putricide: To destroy that which is putrid
Suitorcide: That which destroys the chances of a suitor
Tomecide: To destroy books (especially as in book-burning)

I've a final word in mind to conclude this chapter:

Omnicide: The destruction of everything (as in a nuclear war)

VI

A CONVOCATION OF EAGLES:

Collective Nouns for Animals

Most everyone knows that a group of lions is known as a pride, or that a group of fish is called a school. But did you know that a gathering of eagles is known as a convocation, or a group of rhinoceroses is a crash? Pride, school, convocation, crash: These are but a few examples of collective nouns for animals. Most group terms are familiar (herd, flock, pack, and so forth), so I've limited the following list to sixty of the more unusual.

It is interesting to note that many collective nouns seem to reflect the nature of the animal they refer to. By way of example, "parliament" befits the reputed sagacity of owls. On the other hand, what have crows and ravens done to earn their collective terms (murder and unkindness)?

To help you find the collective noun for your favorite species, sixty are presented in alphabetical order by *animal*.

COLLECTIVE NOUNS FOR ANIMALS

ANIMAL NAME	COLLECTIVE NOUN
Apes	Shrewdness
Asses	Pace

Murder: *a group of crows*

Bears	Sloth, Sleuth
Boars	Singular
Cats	Clowder
Chickens	Peep
Colts	Rag
Crows	Murder
Curs	Cowardice
Doves	Piteousness
Ducks	Paddling
Eagles	Convocation
Elk	Gang
Ferrets	Business
Finches	Charm
Foxes	Skulk
Geese	Gaggle (on the water), Skein (flying)
Goats	Trip
Hawks	Cast
Herons	Siege
Horses	Harras

Crash: *a group of rhinoceroses*

Jays	Party
Jellyfish	Smack
Kangaroos	Troop
Kittens	Kindle
Lapwings	Deceit
Larks	Exaltation
Leopards	Leap
Magpies	Tidings
Martens	Richness
Moles	Labor
Mules	Barren
Nightingales	Watch
Owls	Parliament
Parrots	Company
Peacocks	Muster, Ostentation
Penguins	Colony
Pheasants	Bouquet
Ravens	Unkindness
Rhinoceroses	Crash

49

Rooks	Buildings, Clamor
Seals	Pod
Snipe	Walk
Sparrows	Host
Squirrels	Dray
Starlings	Murmuration, Chattering
Storks	Mustering
Swallows	Flight
Swans	Wedge
Swine	Sounder
Teal	Spring
Toads	Knot
Trout	Hover
Turkeys	Rafter
Turtles	Bale
Turtledoves	Pitying
Whales	Pod, Gam
Wolves	Route
Woodcocks	Fall
Woodpeckers	Descent

A richness of martens? An ostentation of peacocks? A gaggle of geese? Yes, all sixty collective nouns listed above are proper English terms. Or to make reference to the lapwing, there has been no "deceit."

VII

SQUEALERS, SQUEAKERS, AND
CHEEPERS:

Animal Young

Most people are fond of puppies, kittens, and other baby animals. But few animal lovers are familiar with the less common names for animal young. Thus, for the pleasure of both animal lovers *and* word lovers, this chapter discusses squealers, squeakers, cheepers, and other animal offspring.

The young of many animals have no specific name; in which case, it is correct to refer to their young simply as infants or babies. In other instances, animal young fall into collective categories: the young of large animals, for example, are known as calves. Finally, a few select species have distinct names for their offspring. In this chapter, we will first present general terms for animal young, then move on to specific ones for land animals, birds, and marine life, and conclude with a look at words for offspring of mixed parentage.

GENERAL TERMS

The offspring of most species can be correctly labeled one or more of the following:

Calf The young of large animals. "Calf" is one of the most frequently used terms, and it applies to the young of the buffalo, camel, cow, elephant, elk, giraffe, hippopotamus, moose, rhinoceros, whale, and many others.

Chick and Fledgling The young of any bird

Cub and Whelp Two terms for the young of carnivorous animals. Bears and sharks have cubs, while dogs and otters have whelps. On the other hand, wolves, foxes, lions, and tigers have a choice—their offspring may be known as either cubs or whelps.

Foal The young of horses and horse-like animals (donkeys, zebras, etc.). More specifically, male offspring are known as colts, and female offspring are fillies.

Fry A general term for the young of most fish.

Kid The young of goats and related animals (most antelopes and some deer).

Kit and Kitten The young of small fur-bearing mammals. Commonly used in reference to a baby cat, but also applies to the beaver, bobcat, fox, hamster, rabbit, and others.

Pup and Puppy General terms for the young of animals, but especially for dogs and dog-like species (coyote, fox, wolf, etc.); also applies to marine mammals (seal and sea lion, etc.). For a couple of additional (and somewhat remarkable) applications, see the next section of this chapter.

Squealer, Squeaker and Cheeper Any bird young that make these noises, applied interchangeably to the grouse, partridge, pigeon, quail, and others. Squealer also refers to any animal that squeals, whether young or adult (e.g., hogs).

Younglet and Youngling Young offspring of any animal. Applicable to all species, including the human one.

Of note in the above list is the fact that overlap is not only possible, but common. A fox, for example, is small, carnivorous, and dog-like. Its young can therefore be correctly referred to as kits, kittens, whelps, cubs, pups, or puppies.

SPECIFIC TERMS

The young of most animals are known by the general terms described above; therefore, the lists that follow are quite short. Here are the few specific names for the young of particular species.

LAND ANIMALS

ANIMAL	YOUNG
Cow	Heifer (female), Stirk
Deer	Fawn
Dragon	Pup, Puppy
Hare	Leveret
Hog	Grice, Piglet, Shoat, Shote
Kangaroo	Joey
Lion	Lionet
Rat	Pup
Sheep	Lamb, Lambkin, Cosset

BIRDS

BIRD	YOUNG
Chicken	Cockerel (male), Pullet (female)
Duck	Duckling
Eagle	Eaglet
Goose	Gosling

Hawk	Eyas
Owl	Owlet
Peafowl	Peachick
Pigeon	Squab
Swan	Cygnet
Turkey	Poult

MARINE LIFE

ANIMAL	YOUNG
Cod	Codling, Sprag, Scrod
Eel	Elver
Herring	Brit
Mackerel	Spike, Blinker, Tinker
Oyster	Spat (also applies to other bivalves—clams, mussels, etc.)
Salmon	Parr, Grilse, Smolt, Alevin

OFFSPRING OF MIXED PARENTAGE

Closely related to this chapter's theme are the names of offspring resulting from mixed parentage. A baker's dozen of these hybrids are presented below. Of special note is the fact that half are portmanteau words (words formed by combining two other words; e.g., beef + buffalo = beefalo).

For a more in-depth discussion of portmanteaus, see Chapter XV. Meanwhile, the offspring of mixed parentage are:

OFFSPRING	PARENTAGE
Beefalo (cattalo or catalo)	Beef (cattle) and buffalo
Carideer	Caribou and reindeer

Joey: *a baby kangaroo*

Dzo	Yak and domestic cow
Geep	Goat and sheep
Hinny	Male horse (stallion) and she-ass
Liger	Male lion and female tiger
Mule	Male ass and female horse (mare)
Tigon	Male tiger and female lion
Yakalo	Yak and buffalo
Zebrula	Zebra and horse
Zobo	Zebu and yak
Zum	Yak and cow

I conclude with the name of an offspring resulting from mixed parentage but having one notable difference—the beast is purely mythical. Namely:

Jumart: the offspring of a horse and cow

55

VIII

OF CYGNINE MAIDENS
AND ANGUINEOUS VILLAINS:

A Look at Animal Adjectives

Many of us may recognize a bovine person or understand the significance of someone having an aquiline nose. But what do you call someone resembling a bat? Or, heaven forbid, a cockroach?

Words meaning "bat-like" and "roach-like" can be found below along with nearly 200 other animal adjectives. It is more than likely that many of these terms will remind you of particular friends, relatives, or acquaintances. Over the years I have had my fair share of xenarthral (sloth-like) students. (I am reluctant to present this list of adjectives for fear they will find their way into the word processors of genre writers. Do we really want to read about cygnine (swan-like) maidens being rescued from the clutches of anguineous (snake-like) villains? Oh well. . . .)

A total of 184 unique "animal-like" adjectives are presented below. I've divided them into four categories: land animals, birds, marine animals, and insects. Even if you do not possess a pachydermic memory, I bet you will find some unforgettable words below.

Vespertilian: *bat-like*

LAND ANIMALS

ANIMAL   *ADJECTIVE*

Animal	Adjective
Aardvark	Edentate
Aardwolf	Protelid
Alligator	Eusuchian
Antelope	Alcelaphine
Ape	Simian
Armadillo	Dasypodid
Badger	Mustelid (also skunk and wolverine)
Bat	Vespertilian
Bear	Ursine
Bison	Bisontine
Boa constrictor	Boid
Calf	Vituline
Cat	Feline

57

Cattle	Bovine (also musk ox and ox)
Chimpanzee	Simiid
Deer	Cervine (also elk and moose)
Dinosaur	Diapsidian
Dog	Canine
Dormouse	Myoxine
Dragon	Draconic
Elephant	Pachydermic
Elk	Cervine (also deer and moose)
Fox	Vulpine
Frog	Ranine
Giraffe	Artiodactylous
Goat	Caprine
Gorilla	Pongid
Hare	Leporine (also rabbit)
Horse	Equine
Kangaroo	Macropodine
Lizard	Saurian
Marmoset	Callithricid
Marmot	Sciurid
Mink	Mustelid (also badger, skunk, and wolverine)
Mole	Talpoid
Mongoose	Viverrine
Monkey	Pithecoid
Moose	Cervine (also deer and elk)
Mouse	Musine
Muskrat	Cricetid
Musk ox	Bovine (also cattle and ox)
Otter	Lutrine
Ox	Bovine (also musk ox and cattle)
Peccary	Tayassuid
Platypus	Monotremal
Porcupine	Hystricine
Rabbit	Leporine (also hare)
Raccoon	Arctoidean
Rat	Murine
Rattlesnake	Crotaline

Rhinoceros	Ceratorhine
Sheep	Ovine
Shrew	Soricine
Skunk	Mustelid (also badger, mink, and wolverine)
Sloth	Xenarthral
Slug	Limacine
Snake	Anguineous
Snapping turtle	Chelydroid
Squirrel	Sciurine
Swine	Porcine, suoid
Tapir	Pachydermoid
Tarsier	Lemuroid
Titmouse	Parine
Toad	Batrachian
Tortoise	Chelonian
Tree frog	Polypedatid
Tree shrew	Tupaiid
Turtle	Anapsid
Vampire bat	Desmodontid
Weasel	Arctoidean (also raccoon)
Wolf	Lupine
Wolverine	Mustelid (also badger, mink, and skunk)
Wombat	Vombatid
Worm	Helminthic
Zebra	Zebrine

BIRDS

BIRD	*ADJECTIVE*
Albatross	Procellariid
Blackbird	Icterine (also bobolink, meadowlark, and oriole)
Bluebird	Turdine (also robin)

Bobolink	Icterine (also blackbird, meadowlark, and oriole)
Buzzard	Cathartine
Chicken	Gallinaceous (also grouse, quail, and turkey)
Cormorant	Phalacrocoracine
Crane	Grallatorial (also heron)
Crow	Corvoid (also magpie and raven)
Dodo	Didine
Dove	Columbine
Duck	Anatine
Eagle	Aquiline
Emu	Ratite (also ostrich)
Falcon	Raptorial
Finch	Fringilline
Flamingo	Phoenicopteroid
Goose	Anserine
Grouse	Gallinaceous (also chicken, quail, and turkey
Hawk	Accipitrine
Heron	Grallatorial (also crane)
Hummingbird	Trochiline
Macaw	Psittacine (also parakeet and parrot)
Magpie	Corvoid (also crow and raven)
Marlin	Istiophorid
Martin	Hirundine (also swallow)
Meadowlark	Icterine (also blackbird, bobolink, and oriole)
Mockingbird	Mimine
Nightingale	Philomelian
Oriole	Icterine (also blackbird, bobolink, and meadowlark)
Ostrich	Ratite (also emu)
Owl	Strigine
Parakeet	Psittacine (also macaw and parrot)
Parrot	Psittacine (also macaw and parakeet)
Partridge	Perdicine
Peacock	Pavonine

Pelican	Pelecanid
Pheasant	Phasianid
Plover	Charadrine (also sandpiper, snipe, and woodcock)
Ptarmigan	Tetraonid
Quail	Gallinaceous (also chicken, grouse, and turkey)
Raven	Corvoid (also crow and magpie)
Roadrunner	Cuculid
Robin	Turdine (also bluebird)
Sandgrouse	Pteroclid
Sandpiper	Charadrine (also plover, snipe, and woodcock)
Seagull	Laroid
Snipe	Charadrine (also plover, sandpiper, and woodcock)
Sparrow	Passerine
Starling	Sturnine
Stork	Pelargic
Swallow	Hirundine (also martin)
Swan	Cygnine
Thrush	Musicapine
Turkey	Gallinaceous (also chicken, grouse, and quail)
Vulture	Vulturine
Woodcock	Charadrine (also plover, sandpiper, and snipe)
Woodpecker	Picine

FISH & MARINE LIFE

ANIMAL	*ADJECTIVE*
Anchovy	Engraulid
Barnacle	Balanid
Barracuda	Percesocine

Carp	Cyprinid (also goldfish and minnow)
Catfish	Silurid
Dolphin	(porpoise) Delphine
Goldfish	Cyprinid (also carp and minnow)
Herring	Clupeoid
Jellyfish	Discophoran
Lamprey	Cyclostome
Leech	Hirudinoid
Mackerel	Scombrid
Minnow	Cyprinid (also carp and goldfish)
Mollusk	Malacological
Moray eel	Muraenoid
Oyster	Ostracine
Sailfish	Istiophorid
Seal	Phocine
Sea horse	Hippocampine
Shark	Carcharinid
Shrimp	Macruran
Snapper	Lutjanid
Starfish	Asteroidean
Sturgeon	Acipenserine
Swordfish	Xiphioid
Trout	Truttaceous
Walrus	Obenid
Whale	Cetacean

INSECTS

INSECT	*ADJECTIVE*
Ant	Myrmicine
Bee	Apiarian
Beetle	Coleopteral
Bumblebee	Bombid
Butterfly	Lepidopterous

Dragonfly	Libellulid
Earwig	Forficulid
Firefly	Lampyrid
Flea	Pulicine
Grasshopper	Acridid
Housefly	Cyclorrhaphous
Louse	Pedicular
Millepede	Arthropodal
Mite	Acarid
Mosquito	Aedine
Moth	Arctian
Roach	Blattid
Scorpion	Pedipalpous
Spider	Arachnid
Tarantula	Theraphosid
Tick	Acarian
Wasp	Vespine
Weevil	Curculionid

Perhaps you have a friend who is truly inscrutable and cannot be described by any of the above adjectives. In such case, I leave you one final entry:

Sphingine: Sphinx-like

IX

PICK A GOVERNMENT

Living in a democracy, we are periodically cursed/blessed with election-year mania. Occasionally, it all seems to amount to naught, leading people to ask: "Isn't there another way?" Of course there is. Different types of government abound; there is a greater variety than many of us might have imagined.

Words for more than 100 types of government are presented below. These range from "boobocracy" (government by boobs) to "aristarchy" (rule by the most qualified), and many are offered for systems in between (government by concubines, rule by the poor. . .) As you read through this chapter, perhaps you will find a form of government preferable to democracy. On the other hand, some alternatives might be enough to renew anyone's faith in rule by the people.

For the sake of this discussion, I have limited consideration to words for forms of government ending in "-archy" (Greek "arkhos" = ruler) and "-ocracy" (Greek "kratos" = strength, power). This chapter takes a look at words ending in these two suffixes, though not all refer to a type of government (some refer to a type of society, a geopolitical grouping, and so forth). Admirers of dynasticism, feudalism, tribalism, and related governments need not fear—there are regimes here to please everyone. To begin, my personal favorite is

Logocracy: A system of government in which words bear the highest authority

A total of 151 additional administrations are categorized and defined below.

GOVERNMENT BY NUMBER

Everyone knows that monarchy is rule by a single person. Lesser-known appellations referring to government by a specific number of leaders are listed here:

NUMBER OF RULERS	NAME
One	Autocracy, Monocracy
Two	Biarchy, Diarchy (or dyarchy), Duarchy
Three	Triarchy
Four	Tetradarchy (or tetrarchy)
Five	Pentarchy
Seven	Heptarchy, Septarchy
Eight	Octarchy
Ten	Decarchy (also dekarchy, decadarchy)
Twelve	Dodecarchy
One hundred	Hecatontarchy (or hecatonarchy)
One thousand	Chiliarchy
Ten thousand	Myriarchy

Oddly, hexarchy refers to a group of six states, not a government of six leaders. And a "nine-archy" appears to be missing altogether. Once, in a magazine article, I proposed the creation of a word: "nonarchy" (derived from nonary, a notation having nine as its basis). One of the magazine's readers (Leroy Meyers) questioned my coinage. He noted that most names for governments with multiple rulers ending in "-archy" are based on Greek roots rather than Latin ones. He thus proposed "ennearchy" (based on a Greek root). I'll leave it to you to select the "nine-archy" you prefer.

MORE GOVERNMENT BY NUMBER

Several governments are named in accordance with the percentage of the populace participating. If you think only "democracy" means majority rule, then this list is for you.

Arithmocracy: Rule of the numerical majority
Democracy: Government by the people as a whole
Isocracy: Polity where all have equal power
Oligarchy: Rule by the few
Pantarchy: Same as democracy
Pantisocracy: Utopian political system wherein all are equal and all rule
Polyarchy (also polarchy, polygarchy, polycracy): Rule by the many or by a number of persons
Sociocracy: Government by society as a whole

THE GOOD, THE BAD, AND THE RIDICULOUS

Some forms of government listed here seem too good to be true. Others, though undesirable, are all too familiar. The good, the bad, and the ridiculous are:

NAME	GOVERNMENT BY . . .
Albocracy	"White men," or Europeans
Angelocracy	Angels
Aristarchy	The most qualified people
Aristocracy	In the literal sense: the best persons
Athletocracy	Athletes
Boobocracy	Boobs
Demonocracy	Demons
Diabolarchy (diabolcracy)	Devils
Foolocracy	Fools
Heroarchy	Heros

Angelocracy: *rule by angels*

Hetaerocracy	1. Hetaerae (concubines)
	2. College fellows (!)
Kakistocracy	The worst citizens
Meritocracy	The talented
Mobocracy	A mob
Neocracy	Amateurs
Ochlocracy	A mob or by the lowest of the people
Pedantocracy	Pedants
Philosophocracy	Philosophers
Pollarchy	A mob
Pornocracy	Prostitutes
Riotocracy	Violent action and disorder
Snobocracy	Snobs
Strumpetocracy	Strumpets
Whiggarchy	Whigs

GOVERNMENT FOR THE RELIGIOUS

The Moral Majority and its friends would probably approve of the governments in this category. Words for government by religious groups or individuals include:

NAME	GOVERNMENT BY . . .
Ecclesiarchy	A church
Hagiarchy (hagiocracy)	Persons considered holy
Hierocracy (hierarchy)	Priests or members of the clergy
Jesuitocracy	Jesuits
Paparchy	A pope
Parsonarchy	Parsons
Puritocracy	Puritans
Thearchy	God or a god
Theocracy	A priestly order claiming divine commission
Tritheocracy	Three gods

If none of the above are for you, you might prefer living in a:

Statocracy: Government by the state alone (uncontrolled by ecclesiastical powers)

GOVERNMENT ACCORDING TO WEALTH OR CLASS

This category provides for everyone, regardless of his or her economic status.

NAME	GOVERNMENT BY . . .
Acreocracy	Landed interests
Beerocracy	Brewing interests
Chrysoaristocracy	An aristocracy of wealth
Chrysocracy	The wealthy

Dulocracy (or doulocracy)	Slaves or servants
Ergatocracy	Workers
Esquirearchy	Esquires
Lairdocracy	Lairds (owners of small estates)
Landocracy	Landed interests
Mesocracy	The middle class
Millionocracy	Millionaires
Millocracy	Mill-owners; a nation where the body of mill-owners is regarded as a dominant class
Moneyocracy	The moneyed class
Oiligarchy	Oil interests
Plantocracy	Planters
Plutarchy (also plutocracy, plousiocracy)	The wealthy
Ptochocracy	The poor
Slavocracy (or slaveocracy)	Slave owners
Shopocracy	Shopkeepers
Squatterarchy (or squattocracy)	Wealthy and influential squatters
Squirearchy (or squireocracy)	The landed gentry
Stratocracy	The military
Timocracy	1. The wealthy (according to Aristotle) 2. Those who love honor (Plato)

GOVERNMENT ACCORDING TO SEX

Both feminists and male supremacists will find a polity to their liking here. (Note the number of governments headed by women.)

NAME	TYPE OF GOVERNMENT
Androcracy	Government headed by men
Gunocracy	1. Rule by women 2. Rule by force

Gynandrarchy	Social organization among insects in which the male takes part in establishing the colony
Gynarchy	1. Rule by a woman or women 2. Social organization among insects in which the male does not take part in establishing the colony
Gynocracy (also gynaeocracy, gynecocracy, and gyneocracy)	Government headed by women
Matriarchy (or metrocracy)	Society organized with the mother as head, with descent traced through the female line
Patriarchy	Society organized with the father or oldest male as head, with descent through the male line

GOVERNMENT ACCORDING TO AGE

This category is quite small but nonetheless worthy of separate consideration.

NAME	GOVERNMENT BY. . .
Gerontocracy	Old people
Paedarchy	A child or children

IT'S ALL GREEK TO ME

The suffixes "-archy" and "-ocracy" are Greek in origin; many prefixes (hepta-, octa-, etc.) are also Greek. Thus it is only fitting that the Greek forms of government be given separate consideration.

Demarchy: Municipal body of a modern Greek commune

Eparchy: Subdivision of a nomarchy (see below)
Ethnarchy: The dominion of an ethnarch (in the Byzantine Empire, an ethnarch was the governor of a province or a people)
Nomarchy: A province or department of modern Greece
Theatrocracy: Absolute power exercised by ancient Athenian democracy

MISCELLANEOUS

Here are all the unique governments that defy categorization. They range from toparchy (a small state consisting of a few towns) to panarchy (rule over the entire universe).

Archmonarchy: The principal monarchy
Aristodemocracy: The best democracy
Aristomonarchy: The best monarchy
Autarchy: Government with absolute power
Chirocracy: Government with a strong hand (by physical force)
Chromatocracy: Government by a group of a particular skin color
Cosmocracy: Rule over the entire world
Cottonocracy: A class risen to wealth by the cotton trade
Cryptarchy: Secret government
Endarchy: Government from an inner center of control
Ethnocracy: Government by a particular racial element; race rule
Hamarchy: Ruling together (distinct parts have individual action, but all parts work together)
Ideocracy: Government founded on theories or abstract ideas
Jobocracy: The working class
Kritarchy: Rule of Judges in ancient Israel
Merocracy: Government by a part (a partially organized state)
Nomocracy: Government founded on a system or code of laws
Ocracy: Any government, especially one by a particular group
Panarchy: Rule over the entire universe
Papyrocracy: Government by paper, i.e., by newspapers or literature
Phylarchy: Tribal government
Physiocracy: Government according to natural order

Popocracy: Government by Popocrats (Democrats with leanings toward the Populist Party)

Synarchy: Joint rule; people sharing power with their rulers

Technocracy: Government by experts following rules laid down by technicians

Thalassocracy: Sovereignty of the sea

Theodemocracy: A democracy under divine rule

Toparchy: Small state consisting of a few towns

To my mind, democracy is as good as any of the other forms of government presented. However, if absolutely none of the above seem good to you, I leave you with one final entry:

Anarchy (or antarchy, hyperanarchy): No government at all

X

"-OMANCY" FANCY:

A *Divine Guide to Divinations*

In Gregory Benford's novel *In the Ocean of Night,* one of the characters asks her husband for the daily horoscope. The husband, apparently bored with the daily horoscope routine, offers to "nip out for a small goat, put him to the knife and give . . . a prognosis." Such, he believes, is a more "gutsy" form of fortune-telling. Indeed!

Not only is Benford's passage delightful, it also makes two points: first, fortune-telling in one form or another is quite popular, and, second, there are alternatives to the daily horoscope. I have compiled a list of more than 150 of these alternatives, each a compound word ending in "-mancy" (from the Greek *manteia,* meaning divination). I'll grant that some of these fortune-telling methods are a little distasteful, but others do have a certain charm. Of them all, my personal favorite is *gyromancy*: divination by walking in a circle until felled by dizziness (the divination is based on the point of falling).

Altogether, 156 divination words are categorized and defined below. These range from *aeromancy* to *zygomancy,* with quite a few "fancy" words in between.

FOR THE LITERATE

As I would much rather curl up with a good book than put a goat to the knife, I have chosen to list the literary forms of fortune-telling first.

NAME	DIVINATION BY . . .
Bibliomancy	Books, or by verses of the Bible
Graptomancy (gaphomancy)	Handwriting
Logomancy	Words
Onomomancy (also nomancy) onomancy)	From names or the letters of a name (number of vowels, etc.)
Rhapsodomancy	Picking a passage of poetry at random
Stichomancy	Lines of verse in books chosen at random

FOR THE GOURMET

The foods listed here may not be representative of haute cuisine, but they all have been used to tell fortunes. (I keep hoping someone will devise a means of divination using pizza.)

NAME	DIVINATION BY ...
Aleuromancy	Meal or flour
Alphitomancy	Barley meal
Crithomancy	Cake dough
Cromnyomancy	Onions
Foliomancy	Tea leaves
Halomancy (alomancy)	Salt
Oenomancy (oinomancy)	Wine
Oomancy	Eggs
Tyromancy	Cheese

FOR PEOPLE WATCHERS

Have you ever been embarrassed when caught staring at someone? The next time it happens, claim to be an ichnomancer, or possibly a schematomancer (diviners whose methods are based on watching others). There are several additional ways of telling fortunes by observing either people, or their feet, hands, heads, etc. They are:

NAME	DIVINATION BY ...
Cheiromancy	The hand
Chiromancy (or chyromancy)	The hand (palmistry)
Gastromancy	1. The belly, 2. crystal-gazing
Hyomancy	The tongue
Ichnomancy	Traces of posture, position, and footsteps
Metopomancy	The forehead or face
Nephromancy	The kidneys
Odontomancy	The teeth
Omphalomancy	The navel
Onychomancy (onimancy, onymancy)	The fingernails
Physiognomancy (also phyznomancy, (fiznomancy)	The countenance (the face)
Podomancy (or pedomancy)	Signs derived from inspection of the feet
Schematomancy	Examining an individual's form and appearance to infer his personal history
Spasmatomancy	Observing the convulsive twitches of the limbs to diagnose the disease by which a person is about to be attacked
Xenomancy	Studying the first stranger that appears

As a sidelight, it's interesting to note that the vast majority of "-mancy" words actually end in "-omancy," hence the title of this chapter. Onimancy and onymancy (above) are two of the thirteen words in this chapter that are spelled without the "o." The other eleven are: arithmancy, dririmancy, mathemancy, meteormancy, mineramancy, pneumancy, scapulimancy, spatalamancy, spatulamancy, tephramancy, and urimancy.

Also of note in the above list is the term "gastromancy," which has two totally unrelated definitions. The only other fortune-telling word with a similar set of unrelated definitions is "sideromancy" (below).

FOR THE THOREAU IN ALL OF US

The preeminent position our ancestors accorded nature is reflected in the numerous ways they turned to natural phenomena as sources of prophecy.

The following list of "-mancy" words is the longest of this chapter. All relate to the natural world or its inhabitants.

NAME	DIVINATION BY ...
Aeromancy	Air, including augury (flight of birds)
Ailuromancy	The way a cat jumps
Alectoromancy (also alectryomancy, alectromancy)	Means of a cock with grains of corn
Anthomancy	Flowers
Armomancy	Shoulders of animals
Astromancy	The stars (astrology)
Austromancy	Observation of the wind
Botanomancy	Plants
Brontomancy	Thunder
Capnomancy	Smoke
Ceraunomancy	Thunderbolts
Chaomancy	Clouds
Conchomancy	Shells

Myomancy: *divination by movements of mice*

Daphnomancy	A laurel tree
Empyromancy	Fire
Hippomancy	The neighing of horses
Hydromancy (also hidromancy, ydromancy)	Signs derived from water, its tides and ebbs, or spirits dwelling therein
Ichthyomancy	The next fish caught
Lithomancy	Signs derived from stones
Margaritomancy	Pearls
Meteormancy	Thunder and lightning
Meteoromancy	Observations of meteors
Mineramancy	Minerals
Myomancy	The movements of mice
Ophiomancy	Serpents
Ornithomancy	The flight and cries of birds
Pegomancy	Springs or fountains
Pessomancy	Tossed pebbles

Phyllomancy	Leaves
Pyromancy	Fire, or by signs derived from fire
Selenomancy	Observation of the moon
Sideromancy	1) The stars, 2) watching burning straw, 3) hot metal
Spodomancy	Ashes
Stigonomancy (or stignomancy)	Writing on tree bark
Sycomancy	Figs or fig leaves
Theriomancy	The movements of animals
Topomancy	Topography (shape of the terrain)
Uranomancy (or ouranomancy)	The heavens
Xylomancy	With pieces of wood
Zoomancy	Observing the actions of animals

HUMANMADE OBJECTS

Anyone familiar with a crystal ball is aware that objects fashioned by humans have been used in prophecy. Perhaps what many of us may not realize is the extent to which such objects have been put to that purpose.

NAME	DIVINATION BY ...
Aichomancy	Sharply pointed objects
Aspidomancy	A shield
Astragalomancy	Dice or huckle-bones
Axinomancy	An axe-head
Belomancy	Arrows
Cartomancy	Cards
Catoptromancy (also catopromancy, catotromancy)	A mirror
Chalcomancy	Vessels of brass
Cleidomancy (also clidomancy)	A key

Cleromancy	Dice
Coscinomancy	The turning of a sieve held on a pair of shears
Crystallomancy (or christallomancy)	Crystal
Dactyliomancy (or dactylomancy)	A finger-ring
Enoptromancy	A mirror
Iconomancy	Icons
Idolomancy	Idols
Lampadomancy	The flames of a torch
Lychnomancy	Lamps
Pneumancy	Blowing (especially blowing out a candle)
Psephomancy	Drawing marked stones from a vessel
Rhabdomancy	A rod (divining rod)
Scyphomancy	A cup
Spheromancy	A crystal sphere
Zygomancy	Weights

NOT FOR THE SQUEAMISH

Finally we get to the "gutsy" forms of fortune-telling. These are the ones popularized by fantasy novels and "sword and sorcery" movies, and if practiced today, they would certainly raise a few eyebrows.

NAME	DIVINATION BY ...
Anthropomancy	The raising of dead men, or by the entrails of men
Cephalomancy	Boiling an ass's head on burning coals
Crithomancy	Meal strewn over sacrificed animals
Demonomancy	Demons
Dririmancy	Dripping blood

Heiromancy	Entrails of sacrificed animals
Hematomancy (or haematomancy)	Blood
Necromancy (or nycromancy)	Communication with the dead; black magic in general
Necyomancy	Summoning Lucifer
Negromancy	Black magic
Osteomancy (or ossomancy)	Bones
Psychomancy	Communication with spirits of the dead
Scapulimancy	Studying a charred or cracked shoulder blade
Scatomancy	The examination of feces
Sciomancy	Communication with shades of the dead
Spatilomancy (or spatalamancy)	Observing animal droppings
Spatulamancy	An animal's shoulder blade
Stercomancy	Seeds in dung
Sternomancy	Examining the breast-bone

MISCELLANEOUS

The following "-mancy" words defy categorization, but they are by no means less intriguing. There are some delightful entries here, among them my personal favorite—gyromancy.

NAME	*DIVINATION BY ...*
Amathomancy	Dust
Ambulomancy	Walking
Amniomancy	The embryonic sac
Anthracomancy	Inspection of burning coals
Arithmancy (or arithomancy)	Numbers

Ceneromancy	Ashes
Ceromancy	The figures produced when melted wax is dropped into water
Chronomancy	Methods to determine the most favorable time for action
Cryptomancy	Unrevealed means
Geomancy	Figures or lines
Gyromancy	Walking in a circle until felled by dizziness (the divination is based on the point of falling)
Hieromancy	Sacred things; from observation of objects offered in religious sacrifices
Knissomancy	Incense burning
Lecanomancy	Inspection of water in a basin
Libanomancy	Burning of incense
Logarithmomancy	Logarithms
Macromancy	The largest object nearby
Maculomancy	Spots
Mathemancy	Counting
Mazomancy	A nursing baby
Meconomancy	Sleep
Micromancy	The smallest object nearby
Molybdomancy	Noting motions and figures in molten lead
Omphalomancy	Counting the knots in the umbilical cord of her first born to predict the number of children a mother will have
Oneiromancy	Dreams
Oryctomancy	Things dug up
Pseudomancy	Consciously false or pretended divination
Retromancy	Things seen over the shoulder
Tephramancy (or tephromancy)	Ashes from an altar
Theomancy	Oracles or others supposed to be immediately inspired by some divinity
Trochomancy	Wheel tracks

| Urinomancy (also uromancy, urimancy) | Examining the urine to diagnose diseases |

If none of the above divinations sounds plausible, and if you are not particularly fascinated by your daily horoscope, then you might be inclined to classify all fortune-telling as:

Moromancy: Foolish divination

XI

HIPPOPOTOMONSTROSES-
QUIPEDALIAN
DELIGHTS:

Long Words

The term sesquipedalian refers to a long word (literally one that is a "foot and a half" long). In a somewhat similar vein, *Mrs. Byrne's Dictionary* defines *hippopotomonstrosesquipedalian as "pertaining to a very, very long word"*—and that's just what this chapter is about. We'll be taking a look at some incredibly long words from a variety of sources (chemical, medical, literary, and others). First, however, I'd like to address the issue of the longest word in the English language—and it is truly a *hippopotomonstrosesquipedalian* delight if ever there were one.

THE LONGEST WORD

One might think that finding the longest word would be a comparatively easy task: simply look in an unabridged dictionary, find the longest word, and presto—there you have it. Alas, were it so simple. A lot of long words have been cited that are of suspect legitimacy, and someone searching for the longest word must sort through a lot of chaff.

First, it is possible for an author to create nonsense words and to get them published (examples of such "nonce" words appear later). Are these invariably legitimate English words? I should think not.

Second, it is possible to create run-on words of indefinite length. For example, it would be theoretically possible to stretch out the term "great-great-great-great-great-great-great-grandfather (or mother)" 100,000 or more times. But who in his right mind would accept this as a legitimate word?

Finally, there are artificial terms that describe complex chemical compounds. Two such words have gained a certain degree of fame: a 1,913- and a 3,641-letter word have at one time or other been cited by the *Guinness Book of World Records* as the longest English word. However, both share a common shortcoming: they have never been used by chemists nor have they ever appeared in a chemical book or paper. It is true that these words describe real compounds; however, the actual words were deliberately constructed by linguists in search of long words. To my way of thinking, they are thus artificial words and are not deserving of further consideration. Perhaps a similar line of reasoning was behind the decision to delete these words from *Guinness*.

The above is not meant to imply that terms describing complex chemical compounds are not real words. These agglutinative (glued-together) words have a reasonable claim to legitimacy—if they are in fact used by chemists. Indeed, the most likely candidate for the longest English word is just such a compound term. It's the 1,185-letter name for "Tobacco Mosaic Virus, Dahlemense Strain," and it has appeared in the American Chemical Society's *Chemical Abstracts*. It thus may well be the longest real word anyone will ever see, and here it is in its 1,185-letter entirety:

ACETYLSERYLTYROSYLSERYLISOLEUCYL-
THREONYLSERYLPROLYLSERYLGLUTAMINYL-
PHENYLALANYLVALYLPHENYLALANYLLEUCYL-
SERYLSERYLVALYLTRYPTOPHYLALANYL-
ASPARTYLPROLYLISOLEUCYLGLUTAMYLLEUCYL-
LEUCYLASPARAGINYLVALYLCYSTEINYL-
THREONYLSERYLSERYLLEUCYLGLYCYL-

84

ASPARAGINYLGLUTAMINYLPHENYLALANYL-
GLUTAMINYLTHREONYLGLUTAMINYLGLUTAMINYL-
ALANYLARGINYLTHREONYLTHREONYL-
GLUTAMINYLVALYLGLUTAMINYLGLUTAMINYL-
PHENYLALANYLSERYLGLUTAMINYLVALYL-
TRYPTOPHYLLYSYLPROLYLPHENYLALANYL-
PROLYLGLUTAMINYLSERYLTHREONYLVALYL-
ARGINYLPHENYLALANYLPROLYLGLYCYL-
ASPARTYLVALYLTYROSYLLYSYLVALYLTYROSYL-
ARGINYLTYROSYLASPARAGINYLALANYLVALYL-
LEUCYLASPARTYLPROLYLLEUCYLISOLEUCYL-
THREONYLALANYLLEUCYLLEUCYLGLYCYL-
THREONYLPHENYLALANYLASPARTYLTHREONYL-
ARGINYLASPARAGINYLARGINYLISOLEUCYL-
ISOLEUCYLGLUTAMYLVALYLGLUTAMYL-
ASPARAGINYLGLUTAMINYLGLUTAMINYLSERYL-
PROLYLTHREONYLTHREONYLALANYLGLUTAMYL-
THREONYLLEUCYLASPARTYLALANYLTHREONYL-
ARGINYLARGINYLVALYLASPARTYLASPARTYL-
ALANYLTHREONYLVALYLALANYLISOLEUCYL-
ARGINYLSERYLALANYLASPARAGINYLISOLEUCYL-
ASPARAGINYLLEUCYLVALYLASPARAGINYL-
GLUTAMYLLEUCYLVALYLARGINYLGLYCYL-
THREONYLGLYCYLLEUCYLTYROSYLASPARAGINYL-
GLUTAMINYLASPARAGINYLTHREONYL-
PHENYLALANYLGLUTAMYLSERYLMETHIONYL-
SERYLGLYCYLLEUCYLVALYLTRYPTOPHYL-
THREONYLSERYLALANYLPROLYLALANYLSERINE.

In addition to its appearance in *Chemical Abstracts*, this 1,185-letter behemoth has been printed in a *Word Ways* article by Ralph G. Beaman. Mr. Beaman suggests that it be memorized and worked into a conversation. Use it three times, he claims, and it is yours. Well?

MORE "LONGEST" WORDS

If the 1,185-letter word above seems a little unwieldy, take heart; here's a more direct approach to finding a "longest" word. The following are respectively the longest words from the two most commonly accepted standard reference English language dictionaries: the *Oxford English Dictionary* (OED) and *Webster's Third New International Dictionary* (W3).

FLOCCINAUCINIHILIPILIFICATION (29 Letters): This means "the action or habit of estimating as worthless." It should be noted that the word is hyphenated in the OED, but it has appeared unhyphenated in numerous other sources. Hyphenated or not, it's still the longest word in the OED.

PNEUMONOULTRAMICROSCOPICSILICOVOL-CANOCONIOSIS (45 letters): This is defined as "a pneumoconiosis caused by the inhalation of very fine silicate or quartz dust and occurring especially in miners," which is to say that it is a miner's lung disease. It is the longest word in *Webster's Third*.

CHEMICAL TERMS

The preceding discussion should be sufficient to convince anyone that our language contains some rather lengthy words that have come to us courtesy of the chemical profession. A few more are presented here—not with the idea that these are words most of us really want to use, but to emphasize the fact that chemistry is one of our richest sources of long words.

The following are the five longest chemical terms to be found in *Webster's Third International*:

TRINITROPHENYLMETHYLNITRAMINE (29 letters): A type of explosive

ETHYLENEDIAMINETETRAACETATE (27 letters): A type of acidic salt

HYDROXYDESOXYCORTICOSTERONE (27 letters): A crystalline steroid hormone

OCTAMETHYLPYROPHOSPHORAMIDE (27 letters): A type of insecticide

ANHYDROHYDROXYPROGESTERONE (26 letters): A synthetic crystalline female sex hormone

MEDICAL TERMS

Another rich source of long words is the medical profession. We have already seen one example of a long medical word (which I won't bother to repeat); now here are half a dozen more:

CYSTOURETEROPYELONEPHRITIS (26 letters): A combined inflammation of the urinary bladder, ureters, and kidneys.

DYSMORPHOSTEOPALINKLASY (23 letters): The refracturing of a bone that has healed with a deformity.

ENCEPHALOMYELORADICULONEURITIS (30 letters): A syndrome of virus origin that is associated with encephalitis.

HEPATICOCHOLANGIOCHOLECYSTENTEROSTOMY (37 letters): Surgical creation of a connection between the gallbladder and a hepatic duct and between the intestine and the gallbladder.

PNEUMOENCEPHALOGRAPHICALLY (26 letters): Relating to roentgenography of the brain after the injection of air into the ventricles.

SYNGENESIOTRANSPLANTATION (25 letters): A graft of tissue between closely related individuals.

LITERARY COINAGES

As I mentioned earlier, it is not at all unusual for authors to coin new words and to have them published. Sometimes these made-up words become well-known enough to make it into standard reference dictionaries. Others, however, remain as nothing more than linguistic curiosities. The following selection looks at long words of both types, those that *have* and *have not* been accepted by the lexicographers; the former are so noted.

AEQUEOSALINOCALCALINOSETACEOALUMINO-SOCUPREOVITRIOLIC (52 letters): Term invented by Dr. Edward Strother (1675-1737) to describe the spa waters at Bristol, England.

BABABADALGHARAGHTAKAMMINARRONNKON-NBRONNTONNERRONNTUONNTHUNNTROVAR-RHOUNAWNSKAWNTOOHOOHOOR-DENENTHURNUK (100 letters): One of ten 100-letter words coined by James Joyce and used in *Finnegans Wake* (see KLIKKAK ...). This one means "a symbolic thunderclap that represents the fall of Adam and Eve." (Another is presented below.)

HONORIFICABILITUDINITATIBUS (27 letters): The longest word in a Shakespeare play, it can be found in Act V, Scene I, of *Love's Labour's Lost*. It is a word of Shakespeare's own creation, and it means roughly "with honorableness." This word *has* made the grade— it can be found in many dictionaries.

KLIKKAKLAKKAKLASKAKLOPATZKLAT-SCHABATTACREPPYCROTTYGRADDAGHSEMMIHSAM-MINOUITHAPPLUDDYAPPLADDYPKONPKOT (100 letters): Another of Joyce's 100-letter creations from *Finnegans Wake*. This one represents the sound of crashing glass.

LOPADOTEMACHOSELACHOGALEOKRANIO-LEIPSANODRIMHYPOTRIMMATO-SILPHIOPARAOMELITOKATAKECHYMENO-KICHLEPIKOSSYPHOPHATTOPERISTERALEKTRYO-NOPTEKEPHALLIOKIGKLOPELEIOLAGOIOSI-RAIOBAPHETRAGANOPTERYGON (182 letters): The above is the 182-letter English transliteration of a 170-letter Greek word that appears in the play "The Ecclesiazusae" by Aristophanes. It translates roughly as "a hash composed of the leftovers from the meals of the last two weeks" (the original Greek names all 17 ingredients of the hash).

**OSSEOCARNISANGUINEOVISCERICART-
ILAGINONERVOMEDULLARY (51 letters):** Created by English
novelist Thomas Love Peacock (1785-1866) and used in his novel
Headlong Hall. It's a description of the structure of the human body.

SUPERCALIFRAGILISTICEXPIALIDOCIOUS (34 letters): This is
perhaps the best known of all the literary coinages, and it's starting to
make its way into the dictionaries. In case you didn't know, it's from
the movie *Mary Poppins,* and it means "superb."

MISCELLANEOUS LONG WORDS

In discussing the 1,185-letter-long English word, I offered a
humorous suggestion to commit it to memory. On the other hand, here
is a list of words that contains some you may actually want to remember.
The words in the following hodgepodge share two characteristics—in
keeping with this chapter's theme, all are unusually long, and all are
found in standard dictionaries. But you can breathe a sigh of relief—we
are through looking at the hippopotomonstrosesquipedalian words.
The dozen terms here are merely sesquipedalian in nature (they range
from 19 to 34 letters in length).

ANTIDISESTABLISHMENTARIANISM (28 letters): The doctrine
of opposing the withdrawal of state support from a church. It's often
been cited as the longest English word; however, we all know better
after reading this chapter. Variations include the attachment of the
prefixes "pseudo" and "ultra" (see below).

ANTITRANSUBSTANTIATIONALIST (27 letters): Someone who
doubts that consecrated bread and wine actually change into the
body and blood of Christ.

COMICONOMENCLATURIST (20 letters): Someone who collects
funny names.

DISPROPORTIONABLENESS (21 letters): Conducive to being dis-proportioned (mismatched). This word is of note because it's frequently cited as the longest English word in general usage.

GYNOTIKOLOBOMASSOPHILE (22 letters): Someone who likes to nibble on a woman's earlobe.

OPHTHALMOSPINTHERISM (20 letters): The sensation of seeing spots before one's eyes.

PHILOSOPHICOPSYCHOLOGICAL (25 letters): Pertaining to that that is both philosophical and psychological.

PHILOTHEOPAROPTESISM (20 letters): The practice of "roasting over a slow fire" those who have suffered the church's displeasure.

PSEUDOANTIDISESTABLISHMENTARIANISM (34 letters): False opposition to the withdrawal of state support from a church.

QUINTOQUADAGINTILLION (21 letters): The number 1 followed by 138 zeros.

ULTRAANTIDISESTABLISHMENTARIANISM (33 letters): Extreme opposition to the withdrawal of state support from a church.

ULTRACREPIDARIANISM (19 letters): The habit of giving opinions and advice on matters outside of one's knowledge.

This whole chapter has been devoted to a discussion of long words; however, I have yet to mention what may well be a word longer than the 1,185-letter example cited earlier. According to comedian Red Skelton, the longest word is the one that follows this announcement: "And now for a word from our sponsor. . . ."

Can anyone top that?

XII

DO, RE, MI:

Short Words

To counter the effect of the last chapter, here is a look at 139 two-letter words. They are presented primarily as a reference for word game players, but don't let this deter you from enjoying them.

All 139 words can be found in either *The Complete Word Game Dictionary* or *The Official Scrabble Player's Dictionary* (two books that list only those words admissible in Scrabble and related word games), as well as in other dictionaries. Even though some of the following words may seem a bit bizarre, they are all legitimate for use in such games. You may even want to commit some of the more unusual ones to memory; if you do, your favorite opponent may be in for quite a surprise.

The 139 two-letter words are:

AA: Cindery lava
AD: An advertisement
AE: One
AH: Interjection used to express delight
AI: A three-clawed sloth
AK: An East Indian shrub
AL: A type of mulberry

Aa: *rough, cindery lava*

AM: Present tense, first person singular form of "to be"
AN: Indefinite article
AO: A tribe of India
AR: The letter "R"
AS: To the same degree (adverb)
AT: Preposition used to indicate presence
AU: Obsolete spelling of "one"
AW: Interjection used to express protest
AX: A chopping tool
AY: Aye
BA: 1) The bleat of a sheep, 2) the soul (in Egyptian mythology)
BE: Verb that implies equality in meanings
BI: A bisexual individual
BO: A pal
BU: An old Japanese rectangular coin
BY: 1) Preposition implying proximity, 2) A pass in some card games
CE: Variation of "cee" (the letter "C")
CO: Cove

DA: Preposition meaning "of" (used in names)

DE: Preposition meaning "of" (used in names)

DI: Gods

DO: 1) Verb meaning "to bring to pass," 2) the first tone of the diatonic scale

DU: Variation of "do"

EA: River or stream

EE: Eye

EF: The letter "F"

EH: Interjection used to express inquiry

EL: 1) The letter "L," 2) An elevated train

EM: The letter "M"

EN: The letter "N"

ER: Interjection used to express hesitation

ES: The letter "S"

ET: Past tense for "eat" (dialect)

EX: The letter "X"

EY: Obsolete spelling of "egg"

FA: The fourth note of the diatonic scale

FU: A prefecture in China

GA: A people of Ghana

GI: A people of Africa

GO: To move on a course

HA: A sound of surprise

HE: A nominative pronoun for male

HI: Interjection used to express a greeting

HO: Interjection used to attract attention

HU: An ancient people of China

HY: Obsolete spelling of "high"

ID: One of three divisions of the psyche

IE: A type of pine found in the Pacific Islands

IF: 1) Conjunction meaning "in the event that," 2) Noun meaning a "possibility"

IL: Variation of "ill"

IN: 1) Preposition used to indicate inclusion, 2) Verb meaning to "harvest", et al.

IR: Obsolete form of "ire"

IS: Present tense, third person singular form of "to be"

93

IT: Pronoun meaning "that one"

JA: Yes

JO: A sweetheart

KA: The spiritual self in Egyptian religion

KI: Variation of "ti"

KO: 12th-century Chinese porcelain

LA: The sixth tone of the diatonic scale

LE: Musical syllable (scale other than diatonic)

LI: Chinese unit of distance (equal to about 1/3 mile)

LO: Interjection used to call attention

LY: Annamese unit for measuring length

MA: Mother

ME: Objective case of the pronoun "I"

MI: Third note of the diatonic scale

MO: Moment

MU: Twelfth letter of the Greek alphabet

MY: Possessive form of the pronoun "I"

NA: No

NE: Not or nor (dialect)

NI: Musical syllable (scale other than diatonic)

NO: A negative reply

NU: Thirteenth letter of the Greek alphabet

OB: Objection

OC: Yes

OD: 1) Interjection used as a mild oath, 2) hypothetical force of power

OE: A whirlwind off the Faeroe Islands

OF: Preposition used to indicate origin

OH: To exclaim in surprise (either as a verb or as an interjection)

OK: Obsolete spelling of "ached"

OM: A mantra word

ON: 1) Preposition used to indicate position, 2) the stance of a batsman in wicket

OP: Abstract art style

OR: 1) Conjunction used to indicate an alternative, 2) the heraldic color gold or yellow

OS: 1) A bone, 2) an orifice, 3) a long, narrow ridge of sand or gravel

OU: Variation of "oh"

OW: Interjection used to express pain

OX: A domestic bovine animal
OY: Interjection used to express dismay
PA: Father
PE: Seventeenth letter of the Hebrew alphabet
PI: 1) Sixteenth letter of the Greek alphabet, 2) to spill or throw
PO: Impish spirit
PU: Variation of "pull"
QU: Obsolete spelling of "cue"
RA: Obsolete spelling of "raw"
RE: Second tone of the diatonic scale
RI: Japanese unit of distance (2.44 miles)
RO: An artificial international language
SA: Variation of "so"
SE: Japanese unit of measure (area)
SH: Interjection used to command silence
SI: Alternate spelling of "ti"
SO: 1) Fifth tone of the diatonic scale, 2) common adjective, adverb, conjunction, and pronoun meaning "in a manner or way"
SY: Scythe
TA: Thanks
TE: The letter "T"
TI: 1)Seventh tone of the diatonic scale, 2) a type of Asiatic tree of the lily family
TO: Preposition or adverb used to indicate direction
TU: Variation of "thou"
TY: Variation of "tie"
UG: Interjection used to express disgust
UM: Interjection used to express hesitation or doubt
UN: One (a pronoun)
UP: An adjective, adverb, noun, preposition, or verb used to indicate a higher direction
UR: Variation of "er"
US: Objective case of the pronoun "we"
UT: The musical tone "C" (on the French scale)
VA: Musical direction
WA: Variation of "woe" or "way"
WE: First person plural pronoun
WO: Woe

WY: The letter "Y"

XI: Fourteenth letter of the Greek alphabet

XU: Monetary unit of Vietnam

YA: You

YE: 1) You, 2) the

YO: Interjection meaning to commence hauling on a rope (as used by sailors)

ZA: Musical syllable (other than diatonic scale)

ZO: Asian cattle

. . . Fa, So, La, Ti, Do. Ah! That concludes the musical scale started in the title of this chapter. And it also concludes this chapter on short words. Unless, of course, you want to see the *one-letter* words. But that's easy; there are twenty-six of them—each letter is capable of standing alone as a noun denoting itself. O!

XIII

CWM, QOPH, ZAQQUM, AND
OTHER TRW WRDS

If this book has yet to convince you that the English language can at times be rather astounding and that it has perhaps a hint of craziness, then this chapter should do the job. We'll be taking a look at dictionary words that contain no vowels (that's right—*no* vowels). And on a closely related theme, we'll be examining words that contain the letter Q *not* followed by its traditional U.

By calling a word vowelless, I mean that it does not contain any of the letters A, E, I, O, U, or Y. As we shall see, other letters have in the past been used to denote vowel sounds. Thus we will break the discussion of vowelless words into two sections: the first deals with modern words, and the second considers obsolete spelling variations.

MODERN VOWELLESS WORDS

Most, but not all, of the modern vowelless words are simply onomatopoetic interjections (onomatopoetic words attempt to imitate the sounds associated with their meanings). As unusual as the following may seem, they in fact are not obscure words, and most can be found in standard unabridged dictionaries.

The modern (i.e., currently used) vowelless words are:

Brrr: The sound of shivering
Crwth: An ancient stringed musical instrument
Cwm: A cirque (a steep-walled mountain basin shaped like half a bowl)
Grr: The sound of a dog
Hm: An interjection expressing assent
Hsh: An interjection used to urge silence
Nth: Adjective pertaining to an indefinitely large number
Phpht (pht): An interjection used to express annoyance
Psst (pst): An interjection used to attract someone's attention
Shh (sh): An interjection used to urge silence
Tch: An interjection expressing vexation or disgust
Tck: An interjection expressing surprise and delight
Tsk: An exclamation of annoyance
Tsktsk: To utter tsk
Tst: An interjection used to urge silence

ARCHAIC VOWELLESS WORDS

It is interesting to note that the letters V and W were once used to denote vowel sounds; however, this linguistic habit has dropped out of general usage. There are no modern words that use V as a vowel, and cwm and crwth (above) are the only two modern words that still use W as a vowel (pronounce the W as a double-U).

I am indebted to A. Ross Eckler and Jeff Grant for the list that follows (it was first published in *Word Ways*, August 1980). They perused the *Oxford English Dictionary* for examples of words that utilize V and W as vowels. Most of the words they found are obsolete spelling variations of common modern words. The *OED* is the granddaddy of all dictionaries, and these words thus have a certain legitimacy. This does not mean to say that I recommend them for your next game of Scrabble®. If you do utilize them, expect a few raised eyebrows—you will not find these listed in either *Webster's* or in any of the dictionaries of approved words for game players.

WORD	VARIATION OF:
Brwk	Brook
Bwrch	Burgh
Crwd	Crowd
Drw	Drew
Drwn	Drown
Dw	Do
Dwk	Duke
Dwr	Door
Flw	Flue
Frwt	Fruit
Grw	Grow
Hv	How
Hvnt	Hunt
Hw	How
Hwnt	Hunt
Hwr	Whore
Hws	House
Hwsz	House
Mv	Mew
Mwff	Move
Mwk	Muck
Mwnk	Monk
Mwr	Moor
Mwt	Moot
Mwtht	Mouth
Nv	Now
Nw	Now
Nwn	Nun
Plwch	Plough
Prw	Prow (profit)
Pwf	Puff
Pwl	Pool
Pwn	Pun

Pwnt	Point
Pwt	Put
Rvn	Run
Rwch	Rough
Rwd	Rood (a cross)
Schw	She
Schwll	Shovel
Schwt	Shoot
Scwch	Such
Skwff	Scoff
Snwk	Snook (a promontory)
Sprws	Spruce
Spvrn	Spurn
Spwrn	Spurn
Stw	Stew
Swk	Suck
Swlc	Such
Swlch	Such
Swld	Should
Swm	Some
Swn	Sun
Swrd	Sword
Swt	Suit
Swth	Sooth
Thrw	Through
Thrwch	Through
Thws	Thus
Trw	True
Trwmp	Trump (to sound a trumpet)
Tvv	Two
Twch	Tough
Twm	Toom (vacant)
Twn	Tun (a large cask or barrel)
Twng	Tongue
Twrn	Turn
Twrss	Truss
Twth	Tooth

Vch	Each
Vd	Uds (an oath)
Vds	Uds
Vg (vgg)	Ug (to inspire with disgust)
Vh	Uh (a coughing sound)
Vlm	Elm
Vm	Um (them)
Vmb	Umbe (around)
Vmh	Umh (umph)
Vmff	Umph
Vn	On
Vnct	Unct (anoint)
Vnd	Und (wave)
Vp (vpp)	Up
Vr	Our
Vrn	Urn
Vs (vss)	Us
Vssh	Ush (come out)
Vsz	Use
Vt	Out
Wgg (wg)	Ug (to inspire with disgust)
Wlf	Wolf
Wlt	Vult (face)
Wnt	Wont
Wp	Up
Wr	Our
Wrd	Word
Wrm	Worm
Wrn	Urn
Wrs	Worse
Wrst	Worst
Wrt	Wort
Ws	Us
Wsch	Ush (come out)
Wss	Use
Wsz	Us
Xwld	Should

Q WITHOUT THE U

As any schoolchild can tell you, the letter Q is followed by the letter U. Well, not always. Numerous exceptions exist to this rule—as can be seen in the list that follows. I have culled these words from a variety of sources, and though you won't find all of them in a standard unabridged dictionary, they are all nonetheless legitimate English words.

The U-less Q's are:

Bathqol: A divine revelation given audibly
Bawwaqe: An Arabian trumpet
Buqsha: A monetary unit of the Yemen Arab Republic
Burqa: A loose garment worn in public by Muslim women
Cinq: The number five, especially on dice
Cinqasept: A short visit to one's lover (literally from 5 to 7 P.M.)
Cinqfoil: A five-lobed Gothic figure
Coq: A trimming of cock feathers on a woman's hat
Faqih: A Muslim theologian
Faqir: A Muslim beggar; a Hindu wonder-worker
Fiqh: Muslim jurisprudence based on theology
Fuqaha: Plural of faqih
Huqqa: A water pipe for smoking tobacco, etc.
Miqra: The Hebrew text of the Bible
Muqaddam: A headman
Nastaliq: A 15th-century Arabian script
Paq: À large rodent of Central and South America
Pontacq: A type of French wine
Qabbala (qabbalah): Mystical interpretation of the Scriptures; a traditional, esoteric, or secret matter
Qadi: A Muslim judge who administers Islamic religious law
Qaf: The twenty-first letter of the Arabic alphabet
Qaid: A Muslim local official
Qaimaqam (qaimmaqam): A minor official in the service of the Ottoman Empire
Qanat: A type of underground water tunnel dug through hills
Qaneh: A Hebrew measurement equivalent to 10.25 feet
Qantar: Any of various units of weight (used in different Mediterranean countries)

Qasab: An ancient Arabian measurement equivalent to 12.6 feet

Qasaba: An ancient Arabian measurement of area

Qasida: A satiric Arabian or Persian poem

Qat: An Arabian shrub (used as a narcotic)

Qazaq: A bright-colored wool rug (woven by nomads of the Caucasus)

Qazi: Variation of qadi

Qcepo: A type of parasitic infection

Qere: A traditional Jewish method for reading the Bible

Qeri: Variation of qere

Qibla (qiblah): Direction Muslims turn in ritual prayer

Qinah: A traditional Hebrew elegy

Qindar: Variation of qintar

Qinot (qinoth): Plural of qinah

Qintar: A monetary unit of Albania

Qiviut: Wool from the undercoat of the musk-ox

Qiyas: Analogical deduction in Muslim law

Qobar: A dry fog of the upper Nile

Qoph: The nineteenth letter of the Hebrew alphabet

Qre: Variation of qere

Qri: Variation of qere

Qvint (qvintin): A Danish measurement of weight

Qwerty: An informal name for the standard typewriter keyboard (based on the order of its letters)

Riqq: An Egyptian tambourine

Sambuq: A small Arabian boat

Shoq: An East Indian tree

Shurqee: A southeasterly wind of the Persian Gulf

Suq: A Muslim marketplace

Taluq: A hereditary estate in India

Taluqdar: A landholder (proprietor or revenue collector on a taluq)

Taluqdari: A landholding tenure in India

Taqiya (taqiyah): Muslim principle of allowing believers to maintain outward conformity to non-Muslim practices in a hostile environment

Taqlid: The custom of honoring someone by girding him with a sword

Tariqa (tariqah): The Sufi path of spiritual development

Tariqat: Variation of tariqa

Trinq: A toast (used in Rabelais' *Pantagruel*)

Waqf: Islamic property held in trust for charitable purposes
Yaqona: Variation of yanggona (a type of kava)
Zaqqum: A tree with bitter fruit (mentioned in the Koran)
Zindiq: An Islamic religious heretic

One of the words in the above list is worthy of further note. "Zaqqum" is the only English word to have a Q followed by a U *and* a Q *not* followed by a U. Not bad for a trw wrd.

XIV

A PEANUT-BUTTER-AND-JELLY FARNSWORTH:

Eponyms

In a classic episode of the Wizard of Id cartoon strip, the little King speculates what it would be like if a peasant named Farnsworth—instead of the Earl of Sandwich—were credited with the idea of placing food between slices of bread. The result can be seen in the title of this chapter.

Parker and Hart (the cartoon's creators) have beaten me at one of my favorite pastimes. By way of example, what if E.C. Benedict and James J. Salisbury had developed different tastes; would *you* eat eggs salisbury or benedict steak?

Sandwich, Benedict, and Salisbury are just three examples of eponyms (persons for whom something is named). The English language contains hundreds more, and numerous books have been written on the subject. The eponymic origins of many words are generally known. These include common units of measurement (ampere, angstrom, hertz, ohm, roentgen, volt, watt), technical processes (to galvanize, to pasteurize), and the names of specific objects (guillotine, Pullman car, Gatling gun, and so forth). There are, however, many other common words whose eponymic origins are not obvious. I've listed and defined seventy-five of my favorites below.

Mayonnaise: *a dressing of eggs, oil, and vinegar; indirectly named after Mago, Hannibal's brother*

PEOPLE AND THEIR FOODS

To begin with, let's take a closer look at Sandwich, Benedict, Salisbury, and all the other persons whose names are immortalized at the table. Here's a baker's dozen of the best known:

Beef stroganoff: Beef and sour-cream sauce served over noodles; named after Count Paul Stroganoff, 19th-century Russian diplomat.

Boysenberry: A hybrid berry; named after Rudolph Boysen, the American horticulturist who bred them, circa 1923.

Eggs benedict: An egg dish; named after its inventor, E.C. Benedict (1834-1920)

Epicure: Someone with discriminating tastes, especially in food and wine; named after the Greek philosopher Epicurus (341-270 B.C.).

Filbert: A type of nut; named for Saint Philibert (died 684), whose feast day falls in the nutting season. (Also known as a hazelnut.)

Graham cracker: A sweet cracker made of whole-wheat flour; named after Sylvester Graham (1794-1851).

Melba toast: *thinly sliced toasted bread; named in honor of Australian opera singer Dame Nellie Melba*

Loganberry: A hybrid berry; named after its first grower, Judge James H. Logan (1841-1928).

Macadamia: A type of nut; named in honor of John Macadam (d. 1865), an Australian chemist.

Mayonnaise: A dressing of eggs, oil, and vinegar; indirectly named after Mago, Hannibal's brother (mayonnaise is named after the town of Mahon—which *is* named after Mago).

Melba toast: Thinly-sliced, toasted bread; named in honor of Australian opera singer Dame Nellie Melba (1861-1931)—as was peach Melba.

Praline: A confection of nuts and sugar; developed by a chef in the employ of Field Marshal César de Choiseul, Count Plessis-Praslin (1598-1675).

Salisbury steak: Ground beef mixed with egg, milk, bread crumbs, and seasonings; named after 19th-century English physician, James J. Salisbury.

Sandwich: food placed between slices of bread; named after John Montagu, the fourth earl of Sandwich (1718-1792).

ALL THE REST

Most eponymic words cannot be readily categorized. So here they all are, grouped together in alphabetical order.

Baroque: Style of art and architecture characterized by elaborate ornamentation; named after Federigo Barocci (1528-1612), an Italian painter.

Bloomers: Women's wear consisting of a short dress and long loose trousers; created by Mrs. Elizabeth S. Miller in 1850, but popularized by pioneer feminist, Amelia J. Bloomer (1818-1894).

Bobby: English term for a policeman; named after Sir Robert Peel (1788-1850), who organized the London police force.

Boo: Interjection used to startle or frighten; purported to be named after Captain Bo, legendary English fighter of such fame that his name was used to terrify the enemy.

Bowdlerize: To censor; named after publisher Thomas Bowdler (1754-1825) who censored Shakespeare and others by deleting passages he deemed offensive.

Boycott: An organized refusal to deal with someone or something; named after Capt. Charles C. Boycott (1832-1897), Irish land agent. Because rents were too high, the Irish refused to pay; also, they cut off his mail, food, and other deliveries. (It took a force of 900 soldiers to rescue him.)

Braille: A system of writing for the blind; named for its inventor, Louis Braille (1809-1852).

Burke: To commit murder in order to obtain a body to be sold for dissection; named after William Burke (1792-1829), Irish criminal executed for this crime.

Caesarean section: Delivery of an infant by cutting the mother's abdominal wall; named after Julius Caesar (100-44 B.C.), said to be the first person thus delivered.

Cardigan: Collarless sweater or jacket; named after James Thomas Brudenell (1797-1868), 7th earl of Cardigan. (Interestingly, Cardigan also went down in history as the leader of the infamous charge of the Light Brigade.)

Chauvinism: Excessive attachment to a cause; named after Nicolas Chauvin, a French soldier blindly loyal to Napoleon I.

Condom: A prophylactic; named after Dr. Condom, 18th-century English physician, the reputed inventor.

Crapper: Flush toilet with automatic shutoff; said to have been named after its purported 19th-century inventor, Thomas Crapper.

Davenport: A large sofa; possibly named after a 19th-century English furniture manufacturer of that name.

Derby: 1) A type of horse race, 2) A type of man's hat (frequently worn at #1); both named after Edward Stanley (1752-1834), the 12th earl of Derby.

Derrick: A hoisting apparatus or drill tower; named after Goodman Derick, 17th-century English hangman.

Derringer: A short-barreled pocket pistol; named after Henry Deringer, 19th-century American inventor.

Diesel: A type of internal-combustion engine; invented by Rudolf Diesel (1858-1913).

Doily: A type of napkin; developed by Mr. Doyley, a London draper, circa 1712.

Dolomite: A type of limestone; named after Deodat de Dolomieu (1750- 1801), French geologist.

Dunce: A dull-witted or stupid person; named after John Duns Scotus (1266-1308), Scottish theologian. Actually, Scotus was a brilliant philosopher—it was his obstinate followers who gave the word its present connotation.

Fletcherism: Doctrine that every bite of food should be chewed thoroughly before swallowing; named after Horace Fletcher (1849-1919), American dietician.

Gerrymander: Redrawing political boundaries to the advantage of one party or group; named after Massachusetts Governor Elbridge Gerry (1744-1814), who did the same.

Guy: An effigy, but in slang refers to a "fellow"; named after Guy Fawkes, a leader of the abortive plot to blow up Parliament on November 5, 1605.

Guyot: A flat-topped submarine mountain; named after Arnold H. Guyot (1807-1884), American geographer.

Hansom: A light carriage; invented by Joseph Hansom (1803-1882).

Hooker: A prostitute; said to be named after Civil War General Joseph Hooker, who provided this type of diversion for his troops.

Leotard: *a close-fitting gymnastic garment; named for Jules Leotard, a 19th-century French aerial gymnast*

Hooligan: A ruffian; supposedly named after Patrick Hooligan, late-19th-century Irish hoodlum.

Leotard: A close-fitting garment; named for Jules Leotard, a 19th-century French aerial gymnast.

Lynch: To put to death by mob action; origin disputed, but probably derived from Capt. William Lynch (1742-1820), a Virginia man known for taking the law into his own hands.

Mackintosh: A raincoat; named after Scottish chemist Charles MacIntosh (1776-1843), who developed a lightweight waterproof fabric.

Magnolia: A genus of trees; named after French botanist Pierre Magnol (1638-1715).

Martin: A small European swallow; named after Saint Martin (315-397) because they migrate on or near his feast day (November 11th).

Martinet: A strict disciplinarian; named after Jean Martinet, a 17th-century French military officer.

Masochist: One who derives pleasure from injury; named after the German writer Leopold von Sacher-Masoch (1836-1895), who wrote about the subject.

Maudlin: Effusively sentimental; named after Mary Magdalene because she is typically pictured as a weeping, penitent sinner ("maudlin" is a corruption of "Magdalene").

Mausoleum: A large tomb; named after King Mausolus of Caria, whose tomb (erected in 353 B.C.) was one of the Seven Wonders of the World.

Maverick: An unbranded calf, or a nonconformist person; named after Samuel A. Maverick (1803-1870), Texas cattleman who refused to brand his animals.

Mesmerize: To hypnotize or spellbind; named for the discoverer of hypnotism, Austrian physician Franz Anton Mesmer (1734-1815).

Nicotine: An alkaloid found in tobacco; named after the man who introduced tobacco into France—Jean Nicot (d. 1600).

Platonic: A close relationship in which sexual desire is suppressed; named after the Greek philosopher Plato (427?-347? B.C.).

Pompadour: A hairstyle; named after Jeanne Antoinette Poisson (1721- 1764), mistress of Louis XV—who made her Marquise de Pompadour.

Procrustean: To produce uniformity by arbitrary or violent methods; named after Athenian criminal Procrustes, who tied his victims to a bed and either stretched them if they were too short or amputated portions of their legs if they were too long.

Quisling: A traitor; named after Vidkun Quisling (d. 1945), a Norwegian who helped Germany invade his country during WW II.

Retifism: Foot fetishism; named after Retif de la Bretonne (1734-1806), French educator known for this sexual perversion.

Ritzy: Opulent, fashionable; named after César Ritz (1850-1918), Swiss-born tycoon known for his luxurious hotels.

Sadism: Sexual perversion in which pain is inflicted on others; named after the Marquis de Sade (1740-1814), who spent his last twenty-five years in an asylum for his crimes.

Sanforized: Preshrunk fabrics; named after Sandford Lockwood Cluett (1874-1968), inventor of the process.

Saxophone: A musical instrument; invented by Antoine Joseph Sax (1814-1894).

Shrapnel: Fragments from a bomb, mine, or artillery shell; named after Henry Shrapnel (1761-1842), English artillery officer.

Sideburns: Side-whiskers worn with a smoothly-shaven chin; named after Civil War General Ambrose Everett Burnside, who popularized the style.

Silhouette: A likeness cut from dark material; named after Etienne de Silhouette (1709-1767).

Solander: Protective box for books or documents; named after Daniel C. Solander (1736-1782), its inventor.

Spinet: A small upright piano; named after Giovanni Spinetti, 15th-century Italian instrument maker.

Spoonerism: A verbal transposition producing unintended ludicrous effect; named after the Reverend William Archibald Spooner (1844-1930), who frequently made this type of slip.

Stetson: A broad-brimmed cowboy hat; named after hatmaker John B. Stetson (1830-1906).

Tawdry: Gaudy but worthless finery; named after St. Audry (d. 679); "tawdry" is a corruption of "St. Audrey."

Teddy bear: A stuffed toy bear; named after President Theodore Roosevelt (1858-1919), known for having spared the life of a bear cub.

Vandyke: A short, pointed beard; named after Flemish painter Anthony Van Dyck (1599-1641), who popularized the style.

Yarborough: A hand in bridge or whist that contains no card higher than a nine; named after the 2nd earl of Yarborough (d. 1897), who liked to wager 1,000 to 1 against the occurrence of such a hand.

Zeppelin: A dirigible with a rigid frame; named after Count Ferdinand von Zeppelin (1838-1917), its inventor.

Leotard? Benedict? Sandwich? Yes, I can assure you, these were all real people. But if any of the eponyms above seem a little "fishy" to you, then here's one last entry in the same vein:

Guppy: A small minnow; named after R.J.L. Guppy (d. 1916), a Trinidadian naturalist.

XV

OF ACRONYMS AND
PORTMANTEAUS

An acronym is a word formed from the initial letter or letters of the major parts of a phrase. The key element of this definition is the term "word"; that is, the resulting group of letters must be pronounceable as a word. If not pronounceable, the resulting group of letters is known as an initialism. By way of example, "radar" (see below) is an acronym, but "SASE" (Self-Addressed Stamped Envelope) is an initialism (unless you know someone who pronounces it "sassy").

The acronym is a fairly new phenomenon, and the word itself dates only from 1943. Since that time, however, acronyms have become integral parts of our language—as can be seen in the word lists that follow.

In this chapter, we will be looking at a variety of acronyms and related words. They have been broken up into sections ranging from the serious to the whimsical.

TRUE ACRONYMS

After exhaustive research, I have been able to come up with only fourteen true acronyms (words that are accepted as uncapitalized entries by most standard dictionaries). These range from the common (radar, scuba) to the esoteric (alnico, loran). The true acronyms are:

Alnico: Aluminum, Nickel, and Cobalt (an alloy)
Gestapo: Geheime Staats Polizei (German secret police)
Jato: Jet-Assisted Take-off
Lasar: Light Amplification by Stimulated Emission of Radiation
Loran: Long-Range Navigation
Maser: Microwave Amplification by Stimulated Emission of Radiation
Radar: Radio Detecting And Ranging
Rem: Roentgen Equivalent Man
Rep: Roentgen Equivalent Physical
Scuba: Self-Contained Underwater Breathing Apparatus
Sofar: Sound Fixing And Ranging
Sonar: Sound Navigation Ranging
Snafu: Situation Normal, All Fouled Up (Bowdlerized version)
Tokamak: Toroidskaya Kamera Magnetiches-Kaya (Russian for "toroidal magnetic chamber"; i.e., a device for producing controlled nuclear fusion)

FALSE ACRONYMS

The following words have sometimes been listed as acronyms; however, there is some doubt as to whether or not they meet the requirements. In each case, the word's story is explained.

Cabal: An organization of conspirators. Popularly thought to be an acronym based on the names of ministers during the reign of Charles II (Clifford, Ashley, Buckingham, Arlington, and Lauderdale). "Cabal," however, actually derives from the Hebrew "qabbalah," which means "a traditional, esoteric, or secret matter."
Flak: Antiaircraft fire (or cannon). The name derives from the German *fliegerabwehrkanonen*. Since the original German is a single word, "flak" is technically a shortening thereof, and thus not a true acronym.

Mafia: Either a specific Sicilian criminal society (capitalized) or criminal organizations in general (uncapitalized). Popularly thought to be an acronym that expresses anti-Napoleon sentiment. However, this explanation is highly suspect—one reason being that no one can agree on what the initials mean. All of the following have been presented as explanations:

> "Morte Ai Francesi Italia Agogna" (Death to the French! Italy Lives!)
>
> "Morte Alla Francia Italia Ancia (or Anelo)" (Death to the French is Italy's Cry)
>
> "Movimento Anti Francesi Italiano Azione" (Italian Action Movement Against the French)

A more reasonable explanation for the origin of "mafia" is that it is based on the Arabic "mahyah," which means "boldness."

Posh: Luxurious. Many have claimed that it is an acronym for "port out, starboard home" (location of the best cabins on British steamships plying the Far East trade). But this derivation is disputed by scholars, and *Webster's* lists the word as being of "unknown origin."

Rad: A unit for measuring absorbed radiation. Several authorities claim "rad" is an acronym for "radiation absorbed dose"; however, *Webster's* lists it as a shortening of "radiation."

PORTMANTEAUS

Closely related to acronyms are words known as portmanteaus. A portmanteau is a word formed by combining, or blending, two other words. Our language contains considerably more portmanteaus than acronyms, and it is not possible to present an all-inclusive list here. In stead, I've selected a representative sampling of fifty portmanteaus—these include the common as well as the exotic. By way of example, Los Angeles' air pollution is generally referred to as "smog" (a blend of smoke and fog). Since L.A.'s air is not always foggy, its air pollution might be more appropriately known as "smaze" (smoke and haze) or "smust" (smoke and dust). Then again, if I were living in

Fairbanks, Alaska, I would probably want to use still another word in lieu of "smog": namely, "smice" (a blend of smoke and ice). (In case you're wondering, I have not made up these "smoggy" words—but they *are* my favorite set of portmanteaus.)

Fifty representative portmanteaus are:

Agitprop: Agitation and Propaganda
Airframe: Aircraft and Frame
Altazimuth: Altitude and Azimuth
Althorn: Alto and Horn
Ambucopter: Ambulance and Helicopter
Amtrac: Amphibious and Tractor
Aniseed: Anise and Seed
Avgas: Aviation and Gasoline
Avionics: Aviation and Electronics
Ballute: Balloon and Parachute
Boatel: Boat and Hotel
Brunch: Breakfast and Lunch
Camporee: Camp and Jamboree (summer Boy Scout meeting)
Contrail: Condensation and Trail
Cyborg: Cybernetics and Organism
Denim: de Nimes (place of this fabric's origin)
Docudrama: Documentary and Drama
Elevon: Elevator and Aileron
Freezoree: Freeze and Jamboree (winter Boy Scout meeting)
Heliport: Helicopter and Port
Knurl: Knur and Gnarl
Lidar: Light and Radar
Mascon: Mass and Concentration
Moped: Motor and Pedal
Motel: Motor and Hotel
Napalm: Naphthene and Palmitate
Neuristor: Neuron and Transistor
Parsec: Parallax and Second
Permafrost: Permanent and Frost
Petatorium: Pet and Sanatorium
Pilgarlic: Pilled (Peeled) and Garlic (i.e., a bald person)
Prissy: Prim and Sissy

Probit: Probability and Unit
Racon: Radar and Beacon
Radome: Radar and Dome
Rockoon: Rocket and Balloon
Satelloon: Satellite and Balloon
Simulcast: Simultaneous and Broadcast
Sitcom: Situation and Comedy
Skort: Skirt and Short
Slumpflation: Slump and Inflation
Smaze: Smoke and Haze
Smice: Smoke and Ice
Smog: Smoke and Fog
Smust: Smoke and Dust
Squiggle: Squirm and Wriggle
Stagflation: Stagnation and Inflation
Tangelo: Tangerine and Pomelo
Tenigue: Tension and Fatigue
Whye: Wheat and Rye

COMPUTERESE

We are well into the Information Age; some experts have speculated that the personal computer will someday be as ubiquitous as the telephone or TV. The Information Age has generated its own special jargon, known colloquially as "computerese." With the exception of military terminology, computerese is our language's richest source of acronyms. As a tribute to this growing language, I am presenting a short list of computerese's best known acronyms and portmanteaus.

ALGOL: Algorithmic Language
BAL: Basic Assembly Language
BASIC: Beginner's All-Purpose Symbolic Instruction Code
Bit: Binary digit
COBOL: Common Business Oriented Language
FIFO: First In, First Out
FORTRAN: Formula Translator (a language)

GIGO: Garbage In, Garbage Out
LED: Light-Emitting Diode
LISP: List Processor (a language)
Modem: Modulator-Demodulator (device to connect computer to telephone)
Pixel: Picture (Pix) element
PROM: Programmable Read-Only Memory
RAM: Random-Access Memory
ROM: Read-Only Memory

ORGANIZATION NAMES

Citizens' groups have a rather common (and to my mind heartwarming) tendency to form acronyms for their names. I've been collecting such names for years, and here are fifty of my favorites. Most are the names of real organizations, though a few are facetious, and a few more make me wonder. . .

BLAST: Black Legal Action for Soul in Television
BREATHE: Breathers for the Reduction of Atmosphere Hazards to the Environment
CAUTION: Citizens Against Unnecessary Tax Increases and Other Nonsense
CIGARS: Committee Insuring and Guaranteeing Anyone's Right to Smoke
COIN: Consumers Opposed to Inflation in the Necessities
COST: Committee On Sane Television Service
COUGH: Congregation Organized by United Genial Hackers
COYOTE: Call Off Your Old Tired Ethics (lobbying organization for prostitutes)
CRASH: Citizens Responsible Action for Safety on the Highways
CREEP: Committee to Re-Elect the President (Richard Nixon)
CROC: Committee for Rejection of Obnoxious Commercials
DOG: Dog Owners Guild
ELF: Education Liberation Front
FAME: Future American Magical Entertainers

FAMINE: Families Against Meat in New England

FATS: Fight to Advertise the Truth about Saturates

FUTURE: Friends United Toward Understanding, Rights, and Equality

GOOD EGGS: Geriatric Order of Old Dolls who Encourage the Generation Gap Singlemindedly (tongue-in-cheek organization)

GREEN: Guild to Revive Exhausted Nurses

INFANTS: Interested Future Attorneys Negotiating for Tot Safety

LATER: Ladies' Afterthoughts on Equal Rights

LOVE: Language Organization Voicing Esperanto

MAMMA: Men Against the Maxi-Midi Atrocity (i.e., men in favor of mini-skirts)

MATE: Married Americans for Tax Equity

MOXIE: Men Organized to X-press Indignant Exasperation (men against long dresses)

NAIL: Neurotics Anonymous International Liaison

NOSE: Neighbors Opposing Smelly Emissions

OGLE: Organization for Getting Legs Exposed

PAUSE: People Against Unconstitutional Sex Education

PEEK: People for the Enjoyment of Eyeballing Knees

POSSE: Parents Opposed to Sex and Sensitivity Education

PUFF: People United to Fight Frustrations

SAFE: Save Animals From Extinction

SALT: Sisters All Learning Together

SCARE: Students Concerned About a Ravaged Environment

SCOOP: Stop Crapping On Our Premises (group favoring a leash law for New York City dogs)

SCRAP: Society for Completely Removing All Parking Meters

SEAM: Society for the Emancipation of the American Male

SHAME: Society to Humiliate, Aggravate, Mortify, and Embarrass Smokers

SHARE: Society to Help Avoid Redundant Effort

SHOCK: Students Hot On Conserving Kilowatts

SLICE: Students Litigating Against Injurious Can Edges

SMASH: Students Mobilizing on Auto Safety Hazards

SOCK: Save Our Cute Knees (men favoring the mini-skirt)

SPOOF: Society for the Protection of Old Fishes

SUCKER: Society for Understanding Cats, Kangaroos, Elks, and Reptiles

TRIBE: Teaching and Research In Bicultural Education (American Indian organization)

TUBE: Terminating Unfair Broadcasting Excesses

VIOLENT: Viewers Intent On Listing (violent) Episodes on Nationwide Television

YOUTHS: Youth Order United Toward Highway Safety

MILITARY WORD PLAY

If you enjoyed "snafu" (see "True Acronyms" above), here are a few variations you might also appreciate. They are in the same vein, though they have yet to be accepted as true words. I should mention that all of the following are bowdlerized versions.

Military Acronyms:

FUBAR: Fouled Up Beyond All Recognition

FUBB: Fouled Up Beyond Belief

FUMTU: Fouled Up More Than Usual

SAPFU: Surpassing All Previous Foul Ups

SUSFU: Situation Unchanged; Still Fouled Up

TARFU: Things Are Really Fouled Up

TASFUIRA: Things Are So Fouled Up It's Really Amazing

TUIFU: The Ultimate In Foul Ups

WHIMSICAL ACRONYMS

Below is a list of my twenty-five favorite whimsical acronyms. Some are well known, but most are deserving of wider attention.

So if you're RAW, here they are:

ASCOB: Any Solid Color Other than Black

COIK: Clear Only If Known

DEAR: Diamonds, Emeralds, Amethysts, and Rubies

FLAK: Fondest Love and Kisses

FOES: Fine Old Extra Special

GAFIATE: Get Away From It All

GOK: God Only Knows (a medical diagnosis)

GOMER: Get Out Of My Emergency Room (medical slang for patients who seek emergency treatment for minor complaints)

GORP: Good Old Raisins and Peanuts (hiker's trail food)

GRUMPIE: Grown-Up Mature Person

HAND: Have A Nice Day

HAWK: Have Alimony, Will Keep

KISS: Keep It Simple, Stupid

MEGO: Mine Eyes Glaze Over (applied to boring performances or situations)

MUPPIE: Middle-aged Urban Professional (reaction to "Yuppies"—Young Urban Professionals)

POETS: Pee on Everything, Tomorrow's Saturday

RAW: Ready And Willing

SKOTEY: Spoiled Kid Of The Eighties

SMOG: Save Me, Oh God

SNUB: Show Nothing Unless Bad

SWAG: Scientific Wild-Assed Guess

SWAK: Sealed With A Kiss

SWALBAKWS: Sealed With A Lick Because A Kiss Wouldn't Stick

TACAMO: Take Charge And Move Out

TANSTAAFL: There Ain't No Such Thing As A Free Lunch

THE ACRONYM GAME

The Acronym Game involves the creation of "reverse acronyms." That is, rather than reducing a phrase to a word (as in acronyming), in the Acronym Game common words are expanded to a phrase or sentence (with each element of the phrase beginning with the corresponding letter from the original word). The more appropriate the resulting phrase is to the original word, the better.

The very best examples I have ever found come from the charming little *Acrostic Dictionary* published by Reverend Isidore Myers in 1915. In the list that follows, I am presenting a dozen samples of Reverend Myers' wordplay. As you read through them, keep in mind that they are nearly three-quarters of a century old—I am hoping you will appreciate the timeless quality of the Reverend's wit.

Twelve examples of the Acronym Game:

ARMAMENTS: Armageddon Results, Madness And Murder; Expense Nation's Taxpayers Staggers

COMMERCIALISM: Controls Our Modern Morals, Endangers Religion, Constantly Influences All Life, Infuses Strong Materialism

DOLLARS: Dominate One's Life Like A Royal Sovereign

DRESS: Drains Resources, Entailing Silly Sacrifices

FASHION: Faithfully All Serve Honored Idol, Omnipotent Nowadays

FICTIONS: Forgivable Inventions Created To Impress One's Nagging Spouse

GAMBLER: Getting Another's Money By Luck, Ends Remorsefully

GOSSIP: Goes On Spreading Slanderous Insinuations Pleasantly

HOSPITALS: Havens Of Sick Persons; Invalids Their Ailments Lose, Sometimes

LAWYERS: Losing, As Winning, Yet Earning Remunerations Safely

LEGISLATURE: Laws Enacted, Generally In Sincerity; Later, Amended; Then Usually Repealed Entirely

WORRIES: Will Only Raise Rust In Every Soul

Altogether, 178 acronyms and portmanteaus have been presented in this chapter. Enough is enough, but I conclude with one last quote from the good Reverend Myers:

FINIS: Fortunately Infliction Now Is Stopped

XVI

OF LUBBER-WORT
AND NUNCHIONS:

A *Look at Lost Words*

If you don't want to have a gorbelly, you
shouldn't junket. Also, you should avoid
lubber-wort and nunchions.

Over the centuries, countless hundreds of words and expressions have
dropped out of common usage. Many of these were delightful terms and
deserve resurrection. In case you had not guessed, the samples above
relate to just one theme: food.

I would like to think I am not a bellygod, but I must admit that food is
a subject dear to my heart. Here are 100 more of my favorite lost words
relating to eating and drinking.

ON GLUTTONY

Our forebears must certainly have enjoyed eating, if the following
words are any indication.

Bellygod: *one who makes a god of his belly*

Archaic words for gluttons and gluttony are:

Bellygod: A glutton, one who makes a god of his belly
Cormorant: A glutton, so named after the greedy bird
Edacious: Voracious eating
Glop: To swallow greedily
Gorbelly: A big paunch, a swelling belly
Grangousier: One who will swallow anything
Greedigut: A glutton
Gulosity: Greediness, gluttony
Gundygut: A glutton
Gutfoundered: Exceedingly hungry
Guttler: A greedy eater (see Guttle, below)
Lurch: To swallow greedily
Mounch: To eat a great amount
Panguts: A fat-bellied person
Tenterbelly: A glutton
Yaffling: Eating greedily and noisily

NAMES FOR FOOD

What a delight lubber-wort must have been; today it is simply junk food. Kissingcrust, tipsycake, and carbando: who could resist such treats?

Belly-timber: Food
Bouffage: A satisfying meal
Carbando: Meat broiled over coals
Cole: Cabbage
Critouns: Frying-pan refuse
Crug: Food
Earthapple: A potato
Froise: A pancake with bacon cooked in
Gallimaufry: A hash of several sorts of meats
Hodgepudding: A pudding of many ingredients
Hogoo: A highly flavored dish
Juncate: Cheesecake
Kissing-comfit: A small confection used to sweeten the breath
Kissingcrust: Crust formed when two loaves of bread touch in the oven
Kitchenstuff: Fat and grease drippings saved for later use
Lobscouse: Meat and vegetables stewed together
Lubber-wort: Food of little or no nutritional value
Lunch (luncheon): As much food as one's hand can hold
Maw-wallop: A badly cooked mess of food
Nunchion: Food eaten between meals
Opsony: Anything eaten on bread
Panado: Food made by boiling bread in water
Pinionade: A conserve made with pine nuts
Prog: Food
Puddingpie: Pudding with meat baked in
Rosee: A dish flavored with rose petals
Salmagundi: A dish of meat, anchovies, onions, etc.
Sambocade: A fritter flavored with elder flowers
Scandal broth: tea
Shive: A slice of bread
Sillabub: A drink of milk and spiced cider
Sippet: A small piece of bread for dipping into soup or gravy

Spoonmeat: Liquid food; food eaten with a spoon
Succade: Fruit preserved in jelly
Sucket: A sweet
Tipsycake: Cake saturated with wine or liquor
Voidee: A parting dish (consumed at leavetaking or at bedtime)
Whitemeat: Food made of milk

WORDS ABOUT EATING

If munching, chewing, and swallowing sound humdrum, then you might want to gobbet or guttle your food. Our ancestors did. Various words for eating are:

Deglutition: The act of swallowing
Flapdragon: To swallow or devour
Gobbet: A mouthful, to swallow a mouthful
Guttle: To swallow
Junket: To feast secretly
Manducate: To chew
Omophagous: Eating raw flesh
Polyphagous: Eating many kinds of food
Refocillation: Restoration of strength by refreshment
Tiffing: Eating or drinking out of meal time

ON DRINKING

In addition to being bellygods, some of our ancestors must certainly have enjoyed an occasional drink—as can be seen in the following words which relate to the consumption of alcohol:

Balderdash: Adulterated wine
Barleyhood: Bad temper induced by drinking
Cagg: A solemn vow not to drink for a certain period of time
Compotation: A drinking bout

Cropsick: Stomachache from too much drink
Doundrins: Afternoon drinking
Drinkmoney: Money used to buy liquor
Malmsey: A strong, sweet wine
Poculent: Fit for drinking
Pot-valiant: Courageous because of drink
Shandygaff: A mixture of beer and ginger-beer
Shotclog: A drinking companion tolerated because he pays for the drinks
Slipslop: Bad liquor
Snowbroth: Very cold liquor
Sorbition: The act of drinking or sipping
Supernaculum: Drinking the last drop from a glass or bottle
Swillbowl: A heavy drinker
Usquebaugh: The water of life (whiskey)

MISCELLANEOUS

Here are a few final entries: names for feasting, eating companions, and so forth.

Abligurition: Spending lavishly on food and drink
Accubation: Lying down at meals
Ambigu: Dinner in which the various courses are served together
Antepast: Anything taken before a meal in order to whet the appetite.
Aristology: Luncheon talk
Coenaculous: One who enjoys a midnight snack
Comessation: Riotous feasting
Epulation: A banquet, feast
Gaudy: A feast, a day of plenty
Groaking: Staring at someone eating with the hope that he'll give you something
Jentacular: Relating to breakfast
Lickerish: Squeamish in the choice of food
Puddingtime: Dinnertime (time when pudding—the first course—was served)

Simpsonize: To dilute milk with water
Smellfeast: An uninvited dinner guest (one who smells a feast)
Trenchermate: A table companion

In case you have not had your fill of words of gluttony, here's one last entry:

Pingle: To eat with little or no appetite

XVII

THE EYE-OPENER:

Words on Love, Sex, and Marriage

Most people seem to have a healthy interest in matters relating to their libidoes. This chapter starts off with some reasonably tame listings—there is a set of words describing unusual marriages and then a collection of charmingly suggestive adjectives. From this innocuous start, however, we quickly move on to words that are more explicitly sexual (terms for potency, turn-ons, and so forth).

Don't worry, you don't have to be a sex fiend to enjoy these words. This chapter merely acknowledges that sexuality is a universal trait, and hopefully the material herein will be a source of pleasure and not of offense.

MARRIAGE BY NUMBER

Most everyone knows the definitions of monogamy and bigamy; however, few of us know additional terms for marriage to specific numbers of spouses. With the exception of monogamy, all the words

129

below have a negative connotation; that is, they refer to marriages that are not sanctioned by law or custom. Some cultures do sanction multiple marriages, and the terms for these permissible unions can be found in the next section.

TYPE OF MARRIAGE	NUMBER OF SIMULTANEOUS SPOUSES
Monogamy	One
Bigamy	Two
Trigamy	Three
Quadrigamy	Four
Polygamy	Many

MORE WORDS ON MARRIAGE

This collection of "marriage" words is larger than the previous, and it is also a lot more varied. You'll find here descriptions of all types of marriages—the good, the bad, and the incredible.

Adelphogamy: Marriage in which brothers have a common wife or wives

Cagamosis: An unhappy marriage

Confarreation: Marriage in which the husband has absolute legal control over the wife (Roman law)

Digamy: A second legal marriage after the first has been terminated by death or divorce

Dysonogamia: Marriage between persons of markedly different ages (see Isonogamia)

Endogamy: Marriage within one's tribe or group

Exogamy: Marriage outside one's tribe or group

Heterogamosis: Marriage between persons distinctly unsuitable for each other (see Nomogamosis)

Isonogamia: Marriage between persons of the same or nearly the same age

Leviration: Ancient Hebrew custom requiring a man to marry his brother's widow

Mésalliance: Marriage with someone of markedly lower social position

Miscegenation: Marriage between persons of different races

Morganatic: Pertaining to a marriage between a royal husband and non-royal wife, in which wife and children do not acquire royal rank

Nomogamosis: Marriage between persons highly suitable for each other

Opsigamy: Marriage in which one or both partners are quite advanced in age

Pantagamy: Community marriage in which every woman is married to every man, and vice versa

Polyandry: Marriage of a woman to more than one man at the same time (sanctioned by law or custom)

Polygyny: Marriage of a man to more than one woman at the same time (sanctioned by law or custom)

Punalua: Group marriage in which two or more brothers marry two or more sisters (Hawaii)

Sororate: Marrying a wife's sister after the wife dies

ADJECTIVES GUARANTEED TO PLEASE

We all appreciate a compliment now and then, even if it is a hackneyed one. But there is no need to use tired old expressions to express your sentiments: here's a list of two dozen refreshingly unfamiliar adjectives you might like to try on someone special. A few of these adjectives might provoke a blush, but most should be met by a smile (especially once you have explained what you mean).

The complimentary adjectives are:

Adonic: Pertaining to an unusually handsome man

Bathykolpian: Deep bosomed

Braw: Pertaining to a handsome, brave, and smart lad (Scottish)

Bustluscious: Having shapely breasts

Callipygian: Having shapely buttocks

Daphnean: Shy and beautiful

Eesome: Pleasing to the eye
Evancalous: Pleasant to embrace
Exoptable: Extremely desirable
Gracile: Slender and graceful
Kempt: Having a neatly kept and trim appearance (this word is better known in its negative form; i.e., "unkempt")
Leesome: Lovable
Leptosome: Having a pleasingly slender body
Macromastic: Having large breasts
Mignon: Delicately small and dainty; petite
Pulchritudinous: Pertaining to physical comeliness
Sightsome: Delightful to behold
Svelte: Pertaining to a stylishly slender woman
Tawny: Having a well-tanned appearance
Toothsome: Voluptuous and alluring
Tretis: Well-proportioned and graceful
Venust: Beautiful and elegant (like Venus)
Verecund: Shy and bashful
Zaftig: Having a pleasantly plump figure

POTENT WORDS

To start off our look at the more explicit words, here is a collection that I find downright fascinating. In a sense this section might be labeled "For Men Only" because each of the following words deals with male potency in a variety of circumstances.

Idiogamy: State of being sexually potent with just a few women and impotent with all others
Paravalent: Potent sexually only in unusual circumstances
Pronovalent: Potent sexually in the prone position only
Stasivalent: Potent sexually in the standing position only
Supinovalent: Potent sexually only when supine
Uxoravalence: State of being sexually potent with most women, but not with one's wife
Uxorovalence: State of being sexually potent with one's wife but not with other women

WORDS OF AROUSAL

Everyone has his or her own sexual preferences. Perhaps you won't find your favorite here, but then again, maybe you will.

The words of arousal are:

TERM	AROUSAL CAUSED BY . . .
Algolagnia	Giving or receiving pain
Crurophilous	Legs
Erotomastia	Caressing breasts
Hyphephilia	Touching or rubbing certain fabrics (silk, velvet, etc.)
Iconolagny	Viewing erotic pictures
Kleptolagnia	Stealing
Mazophilous	Breasts
Merophilous	Thighs
Osphresiolagnia	Odors
Pygophilous	Buttocks
Pyrolagnia	Starting or watching fires
Tantalolagnia	Teasing
Thelerethism	Nipples
Titallagnia	Tickling
Undinism	Sight of water

PROMISCUOUS WORDS

Here's a collection of promiscuous words, though they may not be exactly what you are expecting. According to *Webster's*, "promiscuous" means "composed of all sorts of persons or things"—in a word "miscellaneous." In keeping with this chapter's theme, all the words below are related either directly or indirectly to love and sex (and thus have affinity to that *other* connotation of promiscuous).

The promiscuous words are:

Agapism: Doctrine exalting the value of love
Agastopia: Admiration of a particular part of another's body

Alarsenia: Lack of sexual desire in males

Amorist: A devotee of sexual love

Anililagnia: A young man's erotic interest in a much older woman

Aphallatosis: Mental disorder resulting from lack of a sex life

Apistia: Faithlessness in marriage (opposite of hereism)

Avirgynia: Lack of sexual relations between husband and wife

Cataglottism: Tongue-kissing

Cicisbeat: Male lover that a wife keeps with her husband's permission

Cypripareunia: Sexual intercourse with a prostitute

Deupareunia: Sexual act gratifying to both participants (see meupareunia)

Dysorgasmia: An orgasm achieved after great effort

Ecdysiast: A stripper

Emeronaria: Sexual daydreaming

Endytolagnia: Sexual intercourse with a fully dressed female

Frotteur: A male who gets sexual satisfaction by rubbing against women (especially strangers in crowded public places)

Gynelimia: Strong desire for feminine companionship after long separation (as in returning soldiers and sailors)

Hereism: Faithfulness in marriage (opposite of apistia)

Hypnudism: The practice of sleeping in the nude

Matutolagnia: Sexual desire felt in the morning

Meupareunia: Sexual act gratifying to only one participant

Neanirosis: Sexual desire for younger women

Neolagnia: First appearance of sexual desire

Opsimatria: The bearing of a child by an elderly woman

Opsipatria: The fathering of a child by an elderly man

Osculation: The act of kissing

Proxenetism: The practice of pimping as performed by females

Pygmalionism: Condition of falling in love with one's own creation

Sarmassation: Amorous caressing of female flesh

Shunamitism: The act of old men sleeping with young girls in the belief that the closeness of youthful bodies can have a rejuvenating effect

Spanogyny: A location or situation that is characterized by a scarcity of women

Syndyasmian: Of or relating to a temporary sexual union (as in a one-night stand)

Synorgasmia: Orgasm occurring simultaneously in both partners
Tachorgasmia: An orgasm arrived at quickly and easily
Varietism: A craving for variety in one's love affairs
Vernalagnia: Increase of sexual desire in the spring

To bring this chapter to a "full" and fitting "end," I offer this final word:

Spheropygian: Having full and rounded buttocks.

XVIII

THE PENULTIMATE CHAPTER:

151 Uncategorizable but Delightful Words

Though this is the penultimate chapter, it's the last to present a word list (the final chapter is devoted to a discussion of word play). You will find here a true potpourri—a mix of words that are not readily categorized. In a way, this chapter is a listing of my favorites. These are all words I liked and wanted to include but couldn't fit in elsewhere. So here they are, in a showcase of their own: 151 words intended to tickle your verbal fancy.

By the way, in case you are not familiar with "penultimate," you'll find it in the list which follows. The 151 favorites are:

Abulia: Abnormal ability to act or make decisions

Acrohypothermy: Condition of feeling coldness in the extremities, especially the feet.

Adipsia: Prolonged abstinence from the intake of fluids

Adust: Having a sunburned appearance

Agerasia: Youthful appearance in an older person

Aggiornamento: Modernizing, the act of bringing something up to date

Ahimsa: The doctrine of not harming any living thing (in Buddhism and Hinduism)

Allonym: The name of a real person borrowed by an author. (Richard Bachman, for example, is *not* Stephen King's pseudonym—it's his allonym)

Ambeer: Tobacco juice

Amphigory: A poem which at first appears to be meaningful, but upon examination is found to be nonsense.

Amplexus: The mating embrace of a frog or toad

Anophelosis: Morbid state due to extreme frustration

Anosmia: Loss or impairment of the sense of smell

Anthropophilic: Pertaining to a mosquito that prefers humans to other animals

Aposiopesis: Deliberately leaving a statement incomplete to imply a threat

Arcadia: An idealized rural locality known for its simple and quiet life

Aristophren: A person having a superior intellect

Astrobleme: A scar left on the Earth's surface by the impact of a meteorite

Bantingism: Dieting by avoiding sweets

Bariatrics: The branch of medicine that deals with treating obesity

Bastinado: A blow with a stick or club, especially one to the soles of the feet as a form of punishment

Beauism: The tendency to give excessive attention to matters of dress and etiquette

Bibliobibuli: People who read too much (coined by H.L. Mencken)

Bibliolatry: Worship of books

Bibliotaph: Someone who hides or hoards books

Blik: A commitment to religious or philosophical principles

Borborygmus: The rumblings caused by an excess of intestinal gas

Boustrophedon: A style of writing (typically seen in carved stone) in which the first line runs left to right, the second right to left, and so forth

Brannigan: A drinking spree

Camouflet: The cavity that results from a deep underground explosion (when there is no rupture on the surface)

Cattery: An establishment for the care and boarding of cats

Chad: The tiny bits of paper left over from punching data cards

Charrette: A final intensive effort to finish a project before a deadline

Cheongsam: Oriental dress that has a slit skirt and Mandarin collar

Cinematheque: Movie house noted for screening unconventional films

Cisvestitism: The habit of dressing *only* in the clothes of one's own sex

Claqueur: A person paid to applaud at operas, plays, recitals, and related performances

Confabulation: The act of replacing memory loss with fantasies

Coruscation: A brilliant flash of wit

Cynanthropy: Mental disorder in which the sufferer imagines himself to be a dog

Dactylograde: Walking on one's toes

Dactylonomy: The practice of counting on one's fingers

Daymare: An anxiety attack

Defenestration: The act of throwing someone or something out a window

Deipnosophist: Someone skilled in making dinner table conversation

Déja vu: Illusion that a situation is familiar, when in fact it has never been previously experienced (see jamais vu)

Dermatoglyphics: The skin patterns on the palms and soles of the feet

Dilettante: Someone whose interest in a particular art or science is merely superficial

Diurnation: The habit of sleeping during the day instead of at night

Dontopedalogy: Aptitude for putting one's foot in one's mouth (coined by Prince Philip)

Dormition: A peaceful and painless death

Duende: The power to attract via personal charm

Duoply: Market condition in which there are exactly two sellers (as compared to monopoly—only one seller present)

Dysrhythmia: Jet lag

Dystopia: A locality that is depressingly wretched (opposite of utopia)

Eidolism: A belief in ghosts

Ejaculatorium: The room in a sperm bank where "donations" are made

Ephelides: Freckles

Esophoria: A type of squint in which the eyes turn in toward the nose

Euania: Ease in becoming fully awake (opposite of dysania)

Euneirophrenia: A peaceful state of mind following a pleasant dream (opposite of malneirophrenia)

Exoteric: Ordinary or simple (opposite of esoteric)

Defenestration: *throwing someone or something out a window*

Farceuse: An actress skilled in playing light and humorous drama

Fardel: A bundle or parcel

Fellmonger: Someone who removes hair from animal hides in preparation for tanning

Feuterer: Someone who keeps a dog

Flatus: Gas generated in the stomach or bowels

Formication: The feeling that ants or other bugs are crawling on you

Gargalesthesia: The sensation caused by tickling

Gemütlich: Pertaining to that which is agreeably pleasant and comfortable

Girning: The act of contorting one's face

Girouettism: The practice of frequently altering personal opinions to follow popular trends

Glossospasm: Rapid protrusion and retraction of the tongue

Hamartia: The classic tragic flaw; i.e., a single character defect

Hypnopedia: The process of learning while asleep (by listening to a recording, etc.)

Illeism: Reference to oneself by use of the third person

Infavoidance: The act of covering up one's inferiority complex

Inglenook: A place by the fire or any warm and comfortable area

Insilium: Legal term for evil advice or counsel

Jamais vu: Illusion that one has never previously experienced a situation, when in fact it is quite familiar (see Déja vu)

Jen: A compassionate love for all humanity or for the whole world

Karateka: A karate expert

Kloof: A deep ravine

Kludge: A system (especially of computers) made up of poorly matched components

Lallation: Pronouncing an "R" so that it sounds like an "L"

Lapidation: The act of stoning a person to death

Latrocination: A robbery that involves the use of force or violence

Lexicon: A fancy synonym for "dictionary"

Litotes: A form of understatement in which two negatives are used to make a positive ("he was not unhappy")

Longueur: A long and boring passage in a work of literature, drama, music, etc.

Macarism: The practice of making others happy by praising them

Matutinal: Pertaining to anything that takes place in the morning

Melorrhea: The writing of excessively long musical works

Meteorism: A tendency to uncontrollable passing of intestinal gas

Metrona: A young grandmother

Microperf: The very small perforations along the edges of computer paper

Migrateur: A wanderer

Mnemonic: That which assists memory (a classic mnemonic device is the one familiar to astronomy students: "Oh be a fine girl, kiss me"—a unique way to remember the stellar classifications O,B,A,F,G,K, and M)

Moria: Morbid impulse to make jokes

Omnistrain: The stresses of modern life

Omphaloskepsis: The act of contemplating one's navel

Onychophagy: The habit of biting one's fingernails

Oxymoron: A phrase or expression composed of contradictory elements ("awfully good," for example)

Pogonophile: *someone who loves beards*

Panchreston: A broadly inclusive thesis that purports to cover all aspects of its subject but usually ends up as an unacceptable oversimplification

Paragoge: The addition of a nonstandard sound at the end of a word ("idear" for "idea," etc.)

Penultimate: That which is next to last (ultimate being the last)

Philosophaster: Someone who purports to be a philosopher, but who actually has only superficial knowledge of the subject

Plenilune: The time of the full moon

Poetaster: Someone who writes inferior poetry

Pogonophile: Someone who loves beards

Polydactyl: Having more than the normal complement of fingers or toes

Polymath: A person of great and diversified learning

Polysemy: A word that has a variety of meanings

Prosopagnosis: Loss of memory for faces

Pygalgia: Soreness in the buttocks (i.e., a pain in the rump)

Quadragenerian: A person who is more than forty but less than fifty years old

Remontado: A person who escapes the pressures of civilization by fleeing to the mountains

Resistentialism: Seemingly spiteful behavior manifested by inanimate objects

Risibility: The inclination to laugh at what is ridiculous, incongruous, or absurd

Routinier: An unoriginal and dull orchestra conductor

Rusticate: To go to the country

Saccade: The rapid jump made by the eye as it shifts from one object to another

Samizdatchik: A Soviet citizen who secretly publishes and/or distributes banned literature

Sialagogue: Anything that promotes salivation; i.e., makes the mouth water

Snofari: An expedition into a cold, snowy region

Snurp: To become shrivelled or wrinkled

Sockdologer: A decisive blow or answer that settles a dispute

Soteria: Possessions that give a sense of peace and security

Subaudition: The act of understanding something that is implied but not overtly expressed

Suggestopaedia: Teaching through the use of suggestion

Suigenderism: The natural tendency of a child to associate with other children of his/her own gender

Tachydidaxy: Fast teaching

Tachyphagia: Extremely fast eating

Therianthropic: Pertaining to the combining of human and animal forms (as in a faun)

Thurification: The act of burning incense

Trilemma: A situation in which one has difficulty in choosing among three possible courses of action (as compared to a *dilemma*, in which there are but two possible choices)

Tychism: The belief that the universe and all it includes is based on chance rather than determinism

Ucalegon: A neighbor whose house is on fire

Ultramontane: Relating to that which is situated beyond the mountains

Valetudinarian: Someone who is overly concerned with his or her health

Veganism: The act of carrying vegetarianism to extremes

Velleity: A wish or desire unaccompanied by action to obtain same

Verbigeration: The habit of frequently repeating favorite words or expressions

Vindicare: To demand or claim one's own rights (in civil law)

Warison: A bugle call for the attack

Wederognomonia: Ability to use aches and pains to foretell the weather

Wynd: A *very* narrow street

Yatter: To make idle chatter

Yerk: To beat someone vigorously

Zoosemiotics: The study of communication between animals

THE LAST WORD

Since this is the last chapter of word lists, this is my last chance to conclude with a unique word. I have pondered the question for some time: what single word is special enough to be the very last word? As it happens, the last uncapitalized word in *Webster's Third New International Dictionary* is appropriate to put a "head" on things:

Zythum: A beer of ancient Egypt.

Too bad the ancient Egyptians didn't have pizza and Monday night football to go with it.

XIX

AN INTRODUCTION TO
WORDPLAY

This, the final chapter, departs from the book's typical dictionary-style organization. Instead of presenting word lists, it discusses various aspects of wordplay. First, we will look at a word game that requires multiple players. From there, however, we focus on solitary wordplay to test your own wit and creativity.

The purpose of this chapter is not so much to impress you with other people's efforts as to inspire you to try your own hand at wordplay. None of the following games requires any special skills, knowledge, or training. All you will need is a pencil, paper, and the desire to meet a challenge.

I should point out that this is by no means an all-inclusive inventory of wordplay. Instead, I am limiting myself to what has been generally accepted as the most popular and challenging aspects of wordplay. If I manage to tickle your fancy and you would like to explore the subject further, I recommend reading either *Word Recreations* by A. Ross Eckler or *The Oxford Guide to Word Games* by Tony Augarde.

FICTIONARY DICTIONARY

Fictionary Dictionary is a parlor game that works best with four to six players. What is outlined here is just the basic game and not its variations (Fictionary Dictionary assumes a variety of names with a variety of rules).

To play: One person is selected to be the first moderator, and he or she picks a word presumably unknown to the others. The moderator writes the word and its definition on a slip of paper, then reads it aloud with its spelling (but not its definition). Other players then invent definitions and write them on similar slips of paper. Once all definitions are finished, the moderator reads them aloud in random order (including the real definition). Players now take turns guessing which of the various definitions is the real one. The moderator loses a point every time a player guesses the correct definition and wins a point every time a player fails to guess it. Each player, meanwhile, scores a point for a correct guess (but does not lose a point for an incorrect guess) and further scores a point whenever another player selects his or her made-up definition. Once the round is complete, another player becomes moderator, and play continues until everyone has had a chance to moderate. At that time, the player having the highest score is the winner.

To facilitate play, participants might consider coming prepared with a few choice words already in mind. The more obscure and/or preposterous the word, the better.

ACRONYM GAME

In the acronym game, common words or names are expanded to a full phrase in which each element of the phrase begins with the corresponding letter from the original word or name. For a more complete discussion of the acronym game and a look at some samples, see the end of Chapter XV.

ACROSTICS

An acrostic is a poem in which the first letter of each line spells out a hidden message. Variations include: 1) having the last letter of each line spell the message, 2) having the first and last letters spell a message (a double acrostic), and 3) having a message hidden in the first, middle, and last letters (a triple acrostic).

Acrostics have been written on numerous themes; however, the two most common varieties either use the acrostic as a type of puzzle or are written in tribute to a particular person (in which case, the hidden message is typically that person's name). It is this latter type of acrostic that is shown here. Should you have any doubt that Lewis Carroll wrote *Alice in Wonderland* for Alice Pleasance Liddell, then take a close look at this acrostic, which concludes *Through the Looking Glass*:

A boat, beneath a sunny sky
Lingering onward dreamily
In an evening of July—

Children three that nestle near,
Eager eye and willing ear,
Pleased a simple tale to hear—

Long has paled that sunny sky:
Echoes fade and memories die:
Autumn frosts have slain July.

Still she haunts me, phantomwise,
Alice moving under skies
Never seen by waking eyes.

Children yet, the tale to hear,
Eager eye and willing ear,
Lovingly still nestle near.

In a Wonderland they lie,
Dreaming as the days go by,
Dreaming as the summers die:

Ever drifting down the stream—
Lingering in the golden dream—
Life, what is it but a dream?

The above is the most common type of acrostic—Alice's name is spelled out in the first letters of each line. Thus Carroll settles once and for all Alice's true identity, and he immortalizes her at the same time.

ANAGRAMS AND ANTIGRAMS

An anagram is a rearrangement of the letters of a word, phrase, or name to form a new word or phrase. According to custom, the resulting anagram should be an appropriate description of that which is being anagrammed. By way of example, a classic anagram is Lewis Carroll's conversion of "Florence Nightingale" into "flit on, cheering angel."

From the abundance of anagrams one encounters, these would appear to be a popular form of wordplay. I would certainly encourage anyone to give them a try, but a word of caution is in order—they can be addicting. Once you have achieved your first success, you will know what I mean.

The following examples illustrate the most common possibilities for the creation of anagrams.

1. Single words, as in: Evil = Vile
2. Short phrases, as in: The eyes = They see
3. Longer phrases, as in: To cast pearls before swine = One's labor is perfect waste
4. Place names, as in: Old England = Golden land
5. People's names (the most popular type of anagram), as in: Clint Eastwood = Old West action
6. Other proper nouns, as in: Western Union = No wire unsent.

Finally, there's one more possiblility I would like to mention. Closely related to the anagram is the antigram. The latter is constructed in the same manner as the former; the distinction is that in the antigram, the resulting phrase is the antithesis of the original word or phrase. For example, my favorite antigram is:

Funeral = Real fun

If you can top that, you should certainly be pleased with your efforts.

CHRONOGRAMS

Have you ever seen an old inscription (on a bell, tombstone, plaque, title page, etc.) in which some of the letters are rendered larger than others and there are occasional irregularities (such as a U that looks suspiciously like a V)? While such inscriptions may appear to be the result of shoddy workmanship, their creator was probably trying to impress the public with his ingenuity. It is more than likely that what you have seen was a chronogram.

A chronogram is a sentence or phrase that contains the corresponding date in Roman numerals. They were once very popular, and literally tens of thousands of examples have been identified. Their popularity has declined in recent years, but I see no good reason for their demise; they remain a highly challenging form of wordplay.

In the classic version of the chronogram, the requirements are few: 1) the Roman numerals substituted for letters can appear in any order, 2) extraneous Roman numerals used for letters should not be included, 3) substitutions are permissible (V for U, I for J, and two Vs for a W), and 4) only standard Roman numerals may be used for the date. In case your memory needs refreshing, the Roman numerals are:

    I = 1
    V = 5
    X = 10
    L = 50
    C = 100
    D = 500
    M = 1000

Now if this seems a little confusing, perhaps the following example will help clarify things. Let us assume an artisan cast a bell in 1607, and wanted to commemorate the date with a chronogram. The equivalent of 1607 in Roman numerals is MDCVII. These are the letters to appear on the bell. A possible chronogram would be:

MaDe for rIngIng oVr father's graCe

Note that the M,D,C,V, and two I's are not in proper order, a V has been substituted for the U of "our," no superfluous Roman numerals appear, and the date letters stand out.

So much for the classical chronogram. A more modern (and to my mind more challenging) version is a form that I introduced in a *Word Ways* article. In this new form, extraneous Roman numerals are allowed, but the limiting factor is that the date letters must appear in correct order at the *start* of each successive word. For example, here is a second chronogram based on the date of 1607. This was the date for the founding of the Jamestown Colony, and I have created the following chronogram to commemorate the event:

Many Daring Colonists Venture In Isolation = MDCVII (1607)

Additional examples of the modern chronogram include:

Man's Creativity Manifested In Impossible Invention = MCMIII (1903: date of the first airplane flight)

Man Conquers Mountain's Last Incredibly Intriguing Impediment = MCMLIII (1953: Hillary climbs Everest)

Man Can Make Lunar eXcursions In eXtravagance = MCMLXIX (1969: first man to land on Moon)

If you think you might like to create your own chronograms, you need not limit yourself to historical dates. You might consider making personal chronograms to commemorate important events in your own or a friend's life. The possibilities are virtually endless.

LIPOGRAMS

Lipograms are written works in which one or more letters of the alphabet are intentionally excluded by avoiding words that contain those letters. One of the earliest known examples is a monumental work of twenty-four volumes by the Greek poet Tryphiodorus. The first volume was written without the letter alpha, the second without beta, and so forth until a volume had been written deleting each letter of the Greek alphabet in turn.

Lipograms have been popular throughout history, and they remain popular today. They can take the form of either original literary works or rewrites of classics. An example of the former is Ernest Vincent Wright's 50,000-word novel *Gadsby*, written entirely without the letter E (published in 1939). Two examples of the latter are Gyles Brandreth's lipogrammatic revisions of Shakespeare's major plays and A. Ross Eckler's variations on the classic nursery rhyme "Mary Had a Little Lamb."

Mr. Eckler's nursery rhymes are probably the world's best known lipograms. Two examples of his work appear below, but first let us refresh our memories by taking a look at the original:

Mary had a little lamb
   Its fleece was white as snow,
And everywhere that Mary went
   The lamb was sure to go;
He followed her to school one day,
   That was against the rule;
It made the children laugh and play
   To see a lamb in school.

And now for a look at Mr. Eckler's variations. The first omits words containing the letter S, and the second excludes all words with an E.

Mary had a little lamb,
   With fleece a pale white hue,
And everywhere that Mary went
   The lamb kept her in view;
To academe he went with her,
   Illegal, and quite rare;
It made the children laugh and play
   To view a lamb in there.

Mary had a tiny lamb,
   Its wool was pallid as snow,
And any spot that Mary did walk
   This lamb would always go;
This lamb did follow Mary to school,
   Although against a law;
How girls and boys did laugh and play
   That lamb in class all saw.

If you're intrigued by the possibilities of the lipogram, I would recommend that you start on something similar to the above before you attempt a twenty-four-volume poem or a 50,000-word novel.

PALINDROMES

A palindrome is a word, phrase, sentence, verse, or longer literary construction that reads exactly the same backward as forward. They have been popular for centuries, and it is believed that they date back to the third century B.C. The oldest known palindrome in English was published in 1614, and it reads as follows:

Lewd did I live, & evil I did dwel.

Not only is the above the oldest surviving English palindrome, it is also an excellent introduction to the subject. The popularity of palindromes probably stems from the fact that they are decidedly difficult to construct. A good palindrome can be quite a challenge, especially if it is of any significant length. Long palindromes have been written (New Zealander Jeff Grant, for example, has composed an 11,125-word tour de force), but the longer works rarely make much sense. The best palindromes tend to be shorter, as can be seen in the following samples:

Madam, I'm Adam.
Step on no pets.
Niagara, O roar again!
Was it a car or a cat I saw?
Able was I ere I saw Elba.
A man, a plan, a canal: Panama.

If you would like to try writing a palindrome, you will find few constraints on your creativity. Palindromes can include first and/or place names, they can be on any conceivable subject, and there are no criteria as to length.

PANGRAMS

A pangram is a sentence that contains all the letters of the alphabet. Some of our more verbose authors have no problem with this: when a sentence is abominably long, every letter has a good chance of appearing. But when the pangram is used as a form of wordplay, the intent is also to make the sentence as short as possible (ideally just twenty-six letters) and to ensure that it has a sensible meaning.

It is fairly easy to make an understandable pangram when thirty or more letters are used, as can be seen in the following classic examples:

> The quick brown fox jumps over a lazy dog. (33 letters)
> Pack my box with five dozen liquor jugs. (32 letters)
> The five boxing wizards jump quickly. (31 letters)
> How quickly daft jumping zebras vex. (30 letters)

On the other hand, when the number of letters drops below thirty, it becomes increasingly difficult to construct a meaningful sentence. Several examples of twenty-six-letter pangrams have been constructed; however, they are considered less than perfect because they lack a clear meaning. Of all the twenty-six-letter pangrams I've seen, my favorite is the following (from *The Oxford Guide to Word Games*):

> Vext cwm fly zing jabs Kurd qoph.

The above means roughly: "An annoyed fly in a valley, humming shrilly, pokes at the nineteenth letter of the Hebrew alphabet that was drawn by a Kurd." As I said, it really is difficult to make a meaningful pangram of just twenty-six letters. But if you would like to give it a try, please feel free—a perfect pangram has yet to be made, and there is always room for improvement.

UNIVOCALICS

Univocalics are a form of wordplay closely related to lipograms; however, they have yet to achieve equivalent popularity. Instead of deleting a particular letter, univocalics make use of only one vowel.

Like lipograms, univocalics can appear as either original works or as rewrites of classics.

The following example of univocalic verse is one of my own creations. In response to Mr. Eckler's rendition of "Mary Had a Little Lamb" without any Es, I present here my version of the nursery rhyme—written using E as the only vowel.

I admit the following sounds a little cumbersome, but the univocalic is a very restrictive form of wordplay. To begin with, the heroine can no longer be "Mary" since that name contains two of the disallowed vowels. My poem thus becomes "Meg Kept the Wee Sheep."

Here it is:

> Meg kept the wee sheep,
> The sheep's fleece resembled sleet,
> Then wherever Meg went
> The sheep went there next;
> He went where she heeded her texts,
> The precedent he neglected;
> The pre-teens felt deep cheer
> When the sheep entered there.

Should the above inspire you to create your own univocalics, there remain to be seen versions using only A, I, O, U, or Y. Here is a starter: "Martha had a small lamb . . ."

CONCLUSION

I've very much enjoyed researching and writing this dictionary, and I am a little reluctant to see it end. But, of course, end it must. I bring this chapter and the book itself to conclusion with one last tidbit of wordplay.

In the acronyming tradition of Reverend Myers, all I have left to say is:

This Humble Educational Endeavor Now Desists

The End

BIBLIOGRAPHY

The following references were consulted in the course of writing this dictionary, and every word listed herein can be found in one or more of these publications. Of particular note is the penultimate entry: *Word Ways: The Journal of Recreational Linguistics*. I have perused eighteen years' worth of issues, and I would like to acknowledge this journal as one of my most significant sources.

Allen, F. Sturges. *Allen's Synonyms and Antonyms*. New York: Barnes and Noble, 1972.

Augarde, Tony. *The Oxford Guide to Word Games*. Oxford: Oxford University Press, 1984.

Barnhart, Clarence L., et al. *The Barnhart Dictionary of New English Since 1963*. New York: Barnhart/Harper & Row, 1973.

Barnhart, Clarence L., et al. *The Second Barnhart Dictionary of New English*. New York: Barnhart/Harper & Row, 1980.

Bernstein, Theodore M. *Bernstein's Reverse Dictionary*. New York: Times Books, 1975.

Black, Henry Campbell. *Black's Law Dictionary*. St. Paul, MN: West Publishing Co., 1979.

Borgmann, Dmitri A. *Language on Vacation*. New York: Charles Scribner's Sons, 1965.

Bowler, Peter. *The Superior Person's Book of Words*. Boston: David R. Godine, 1985.

Brandreth, Gyles. *The Joy of Lex*. New York: William Morrow and Company, 1980.

Brandreth, Gyles. *More Joy of Lex*. New York: William Morrow and Company, 1982.

Brown, A.F. *Normal and Reverse English Word List*. Philadelphia: University of Pennsylvania, 1963.

Chapman, Robert L. *Roget's International Thesaurus*, 4th ed. New York: Thomas Y. Crowell, Publishers, 1977.

Ciardi, John. *A Browser's Dictionary and Native's Guide to the Unknown American Language*. New York: Harper & Row, 1980.

Ciardi, John. *A Second Browser's Dictionary*. New York: Harper & Row, 1983.

Crowley, Ellen T., ed. *Acronyms, Initialisms, & Abbreviations Dictionary*, 7th ed. Detroit: Gale Research Company, 1980.

de Sola, Ralph. *Abbreviations Dictionary*. New York: Elsevier, 1978.

Dickson, Paul. *Words*. New York: Delacorte Press, 1982.

Dorland's Illustrated Medical Dictionary, 23rd & 26th editions. Philadelphia: W.B. Saunders Co., 1957 & 1981.

duGran, Claurene. *Wordsmanship: A Dictionary*. New York: Pocket Books, 1981.

Eckler, A. Ross. *Word Recreations: Games and Diversions from "Word Ways."* New York: Dover Publications, 1979.

Edwards, Gillian. *Uncumber and Pantaloon: Some Words with Stories*. London: Geoffrey Bles, 1968.

English, Horace B. and English, Ava Champney. *A Comprehensive Dictionary of Psychological and Psychoanalytical Terms*. New York: David McKay Company, 1958.

Espy, Willard R. *The Game of Words*. New York: Bramhall House, 1972.

Espy, Willard R. *O Thou Improper, Thou Uncommon Noun*. New York: Clarkson N. Potter, 1978.

Freeman, Michael, ed. *Walker's Rhyming Dictionary of the English Language*. London: Routledge and Kegan Paul, 1983.

Funk, Charles Earle and Funk, Charles Earle, Jr. *Horsefeathers and Other Curious Words*. New York: Harper & Brothers, 1958.

Funk, Wilfred. *Word Origins and Their Romantic Stories*. New York: Bell Publishing Company, 1978.

Gilbar, Steven. *The Book Book*. New York: St. Martin's Press, 1981.

Goldenson, Robert M. *Longman Dictionary of Psychology and Psychiatry*. New York: Longman, 1984.

Grose, Francis. *A Provincial Glossary* (1787). Menston, England: The Scholar Press Limited, 1968.

Heifetz, Josefa. *Mrs. Byrne's Dictionary of Unusual, Obscure, and Preposterous Words*. Secaucus, NJ: University Books, 1974.

Hendrickson, Robert. *The Literary Life and Other Curiosities*. London: Penguin Books, 1982.

Herbst, Richard C. *Herbst's Backword Dictionary for Puzzled People*. New York: Alamo Publishing Company, 1979.

Hinsie, Leland E. and Campbell, Robert J. *Psychiatric Dictionary*, 4th ed. New York: Oxford University Press, 1977.

Hook, J.N. *The Grand Panjandrum and 1,999 Other Rare, Useful, and Delightful Words and Expressions*. New York: Macmillan Publishing Co., 1980.

Hunt, Cecil. *Word Origins: The Romance of Language*. New York: Philosophical Library, 1962.

Kilduff, Edward Jones. *Words and Human Nature: How to Choose and Use Effective Words*. New York: Harper & Brothers, 1941.

Lane, Hana Umlauf, ed. *The World Almanac and Book of Facts: 1983*. New York: Newspaper Enterprise Association, 1981.

Lemay, Harold; Lerner, Sid and Taylor, Marian. *New Words Dictionary*. New York: Ballantine Books, 1985.

Lipton, James. *An Exaltation of Larks*. London: Penguin Books, 1977.

Mager, N.H. and S.K. *The Morrow Book of New Words*. New York: William Morrow and Company, 1982.

Maleska, Eugene T. *A Pleasure in Words*. New York: Simon and Schuster, 1981.

Mayhew, Rev. A.L. and Skeat, Rev. Walter W. *A Concise Dictionary of Middle English*. Oxford: The Clarendon Press, 1887.

McAdam, E.L., Jr. and Milne, George. *Samuel Johnson's Dictionary: A Modern Selection*. New York: Pantheon Books, 1964.

McWhirter, Norris, ed. *1986 Guinness Book of World Records*. New York: Sterling Publishing Co., 1985.

Mencken, H.L. *The American Language*. New York: Alfred A. Knopf, 1963.

Merriam. *The Official Scrabble Players Dictionary*. Springfield, MA: G. & C. Merriam Company, 1978.

Merriam-Webster (Neilson, William Allan, ed.). *Webster's New International Dictionary of the English Language*, 2nd ed. Springfield, MA: G. & C. Merriam Company, 1952.

Merriam-Webster. *Webster's Official Crossword Puzzle Dictionary*. Springfield, MA: Merriam-Webster, Inc., 1981.

Merriam-Webster (Gove, Philip Babcock, ed.). *Webster's Third New International Dictionary*. Springfield, MA: G. & C. Merriam Company, 1981.

Merriam-Webster. *9,000 Words: A Supplement to Webster's Third New International Dictionary*. Springfield, MA: Merriam-Webster, 1983.

Merriam-Webster. *Webster's Ninth New Collegiate Dictionary*. Springfield, MA: Merriam-Webster, 1985.

Myers, Rev. Isidore. *Acrostic Dictionary: The Face Value of Words*. Los Angeles: 1915.

National Library. *Termination Dictionary*. New York: National Library Publications, 1971.

National Library. *Group Terms*. New York: National Library Publications, 1979.

Nurnberg, Maxwell. *I Always Look Up the Word Egregious*. Englewood Cliffs, NJ: Prentice-Hall, 1981.

Oxford. *The Compact Edition of the Oxford English Dictionary*. Oxford: Oxford University Press, 1971.

Parks, Betsy M. *The Dictionary of Initials*. Secaucus, NJ: Citadel Press, 1981.

Parlett, David. *Botticelli and Beyond: Over 100 of the World's Best Word Games*. New York: Pantheon Books, 1981.

Partridge, Eric, ed. *A Classical Dictionary of the Vulgar Tongue by Captain Francis Grose*. New York: Barnes & Noble, 1963.

Porter, Kent. *The New American Computer Dictionary*. New York: New American Library, 1985.

Pulliam, Tom and Carruth, Gorton. *The Complete Word Game Dictionary*. New York: Facts On File Publications, 1984.

Rocke, Russell. *The Grandiloquent Dictionary*. Englewood Cliffs, NJ: Prentice-Hall, 1972.

Room, Adrian. *Room's Dictionary of Confusibles*. London: Routledge and Kegan Paul, 1979.

Room, Adrian. *Room's Dictionary of Distinguishables*. Boston: Routledge and Kegan Paul, 1981.

Schmidt, J.E. *Reversicon: A Medical Word Finder*. Springfield, IL: Charles C. Thomas, 1958.

Sherk, William. *500 Years of New Words*. Garden City, NY: Doubleday and Company, 1983.

Shipley, Joseph T. *Dictionary of Early English*. Totowa, NJ: Littlefield, Adams, and Co., 1968.

Sisson, A.F. *Sisson's Word and Expression Locator*. West Nyack, NY: Parker Publishing Company, 1966.

Skeats, Rev. Walter W. *An Etymological Dictionary of the English Language*, 1879 ed. London: Oxford University Press, 1953.

Sperling, Susan Kelz. *Poplollies and Bellibones: A Celebration of Lost Words*. London: Penguin Books, 1977.

Sperling, Susan Kelz. *Tenderfeet and Ladyfingers: A Visceral Approach to Words and their Origins*. London: Penguin Books, 1981.

Stein, Jess and Urdang, Laurence, eds. *The Random House Dictionary of the English Language*. New York: Random House, 1981.

Thomas, Clayton L., ed. *Taber's Cyclopedic Medical Dictionary*. Philadelphia: F.A. Davis Co., 1977.

Train, John. *Remarkable Words with Astonishing Origins*. New York: Clarkson N. Potter, 1980.

Tuazon, Redentor Ma & Schaffer, Edy Garcia. *The New A - Z Crossword Dictionary*. New York: Avon Books, 1973.

Tweeney, C.F. and Hughes, L.E.C. *Chambers's Technical Dictionary*, 3rd ed. New York: The Macmillan Company, 1958.

Urdang, Laurence, ed. *Modifiers*. Detroit: Gale Research Company, 1982.

Urdang, Laurence. *-Ologies and -Isms: A Thematic Dictionary*. Detroit: Gale Research Company, 1981.

Versand, Kenneth. *Polyglot's Lexicon: 1943-1966*. New York: Links Books, 1973.

Wallechinsky, David and Wallace, Irving. *The People's Almanac*. Garden City, NY: Doubleday and Company, 1975.

Webster, Noah. *A Compendious Dictionary of the English Language* (1806). New York: Crown Publishers, 1970.

Williams & Wilkins. *Stedman's Medical Dictionary*, 23rd and 24th editions. Baltimore: Williams & Wilkins Company, 1976 and 1982.

Wolk, Allan. *Everyday Words from Names of People and Places*. New York: Elsevier/Nelson Books, 1980.

Word Ways: The Journal of Recreational Linguistics. Spring Valley Road, Morristown, NJ 07960, numerous issues: 1968-1985.

Worth, Fred L. *The Complete Unabridged Super Trivia Encyclopedia*. New York: Warner Books, 1977.